A Fan's P

2

A Fan's Perspective

One Man's Exploration of British Wrestling

By Oliver Newman

Published by Oliver Newman
The publisher may be contacted on twitter.com/brummieol,
facebook.com/AFansPerspectiveUK and/or a-fans-
perspective@outlook.com

Copyright © Oliver Newman 2016
All Rights Reserved.

Cover design by Dan Barnes

ISBN: 978-1537232676

The right of Oliver Newman to be identified as the author of this work has been asserted by him in accordance with the Copyright, Designs and Patents Act 1988.

All opinions in this work are the author's own unless otherwise stated. The events mentioned in this work were attended by the author and he holds no affiliation to any governing body.

You may not copy, store, distribute, transmit, reproduce or otherwise make available this work (or any part of it) in any form, or by any means (electronic, digital, optical, mechanical, photocopy, recording or otherwise), without the prior written permission of the publisher. Any person who does any unauthorised act in relation to this publication may be liable to criminal prosecution.

ACKNOWLEDGMENTS

A huge thank you to all of the professional wrestlers in this book that made me want to write about Professional Wrestling in the first place. Thank you to all the people who gave me feedback over the years – you gave me the motivation to continue. To Ric Gillespie for being one of my biggest supporters who believed in me and publicised my work.

To Authors - Lance Storm, John Lister and Greg Lambert for making me believe this book was possible. To Dan – thank you for the Book Cover, To Dave – thank you for your kind words, encouragement, formatting & editing work and last but by no means least thank you to Emma for her Proof Reading. Thank you all.

DEDICATIONS

To all my Family and Friends (you know who you are) thank you for believing in me since Day One. For supporting me through thick and thin and for giving me the strength and belief to carry on my work through good and bad times. Thank you all.

CONTENTS

Acknowledgments...............................5
Dedications..6

1, Uncharted Waters…….......................... 9
2, Promotions……………………………….. 11
3, 2001 – Talksport………………....……... 13
4, 2002……………………………………….. 15
5, 2003…………………………………………17
6, 2004 – The Wrestling Channel………….. 18
7, 2005 – The Year of the Supershows……..20
8, 2006……………………………………….. 25
9, 2007 – Taking a Closer Look at British Wrestling
…………………………………………………... 35
10, The Return……………………………….. 44
11, October 2007…………………………….115
12, November 2007………………………….179
13, December 2007………………………….. 211
14, What a way to end the year!......................243

About the Author……………………………... 244

8

1. UNCHARTED WATERS

It's 29th March 2016 - I'm sitting here with no job and an unsure future, so with nothing to lose I'm going to take a trip into uncharted waters.

After WWE Summerslam (of this year) I will have been watching professional wrestling for a quarter of a century. After my Birthday – 31st May (of this year) I will have been writing about professional wrestling for 12 years.

For the longest time I had thought and dreamt about this moment, hoping to become someone in life so I could write an autobiography that people would care enough about to read. This isn't an autobiography, I hope to write that at a later point in life.

This book chronicles my journey from hearing professional wrestling being talked about on radio (via Talksport in the UK) and the subsequent Frontier Wrestling Alliance's 'Revival' to my first ever live British professional wrestling show, the impact that had on me and the first number of months of my almost two year quest to prove to everyone in the world that British Wrestling was as good if not better than it's counter parts (in the US, Japan and beyond).

I remember vividly watching professional wrestling for the first time in August 1991 (26th August 1991) to be exact. The event was WWE Summerslam and the match I remember (clear as day) was Bret 'The Hitman' Hart vs Mr. Perfect (c) for the W.W.E. Intercontinental Title. What I witnessed was a pro wrestling masterpiece (my seven year old) self didn't know that at the time – but this match has gone down in the annals of history in W.W.E.

I disliked Perfect's cockiness and arrogance (I would later on learn to love it) and rallied behind the man who would become my favourite all-time professional wrestler in Bret Hart and when he pulled off the upset win (at the time) I was to experience my first ever joyful pro wrestling moment.

At the beginning of 1992 I watched in complete awe and amazement as The Rockers (Marty Jannetty and Shawn Michaels) split up in Brutus 'The Barber' Beefcake's 'Barbershop' – Michaels putting Jannetty's face through the Barbershop window was/is one of the most real moments I have ever witnessed as a professional wrestling fan.

Wrestlemania 8 is the moment/event that cemented my love of professional wrestling - a good card from top to bottom highlighted by excellent matches in the form of Bret 'The Hitman' Hart vs 'Rowdy' Roddy Piper (c) for the WWE I.C. Title and 'Macho Man' Randy Savage vs Ric Flair (c) for the WWE Title.

2. PROMOTIONS

FWA – Frontier Wrestling Alliance – aimed mostly at the 18-30 demographic.

ROH – Ring of Honor – aimed mostly at the 18-30 demographic.

CZW – Combat Zone Wrestling – aimed mostly at the 18-30 demographic who enjoy the hardcore/ultraviolent style of wrestling.

WWE – World Wrestling Entertainment – Although it has a PG Rating, it covers the widest demographic, it appeals to young and old alike.

1PW – One Pro Wrestling – aimed mostly at the 18-30 demographic, although there has been plenty of families present at shows.

TBW – Total Brutality Wrestling – despite the second word in the promotion name, this was a family friendly promotion.

LPW – Leicester Pro Wrestling – Family friendly professional wrestling.

AWW – Anti Watershed Wrestling – Although they aimed for the 18-30 demographic, there was plenty of families present at shows.

ASW – All Star Wrestling – Family friendly professional wrestling.

WAR – Wrestling Association of Rugby – Family friendly professional wrestling.

Triple X Wrestling – aimed at the 18-30 demographic.

LWL – Legends Wrestling League – Family friendly professional wrestling.

NBW – Norton British Wrestling - Family friendly professional wrestling.

Celtic Wrestling – Family friendly professional wrestling.

Slam Wrestling – Family friendly professional wrestling.

Power Trip Wrestling – Family friendly professional wrestling.

Sovereign World Wrestling Alliance – Family friendly professional wrestling.

Future Championship Wrestling – Family friendly professional wrestling with a slight nod towards the 18-30 demographic.

Extreme 2 Wrestling – Family friendly professional wrestling.

With all that being said I have edited this book so it can be read by all age groups.

3. 2001
TALKSPORT

In 2001 after doing some radio station searching I came across Talksport radio show where I would hear the voice of 'The Showstealer' Alex Shane for the first time. I was impressed by Shane's passion and knowledge of pro wrestling and I was amazed that there was a radio station in the UK that talked about professional wrestling.

From here I would listen every Saturday and eventually heard about a show being promoted called FWA 'Revival' featuring a King Of England tournament - it was to take place at Crystal Palace Indoor Arena, London, England on Saturday 9th February 2002.

It was during December of this year (1st December 2001 to be exact) that I would go to my first ever live professional wrestling event World Wrestling Allstars in my hometown of Birmingham, England with my Brother. I saw the show being mentioned and pleaded with my Dad, to buy us tickets to the show, asking him to ring as soon as they went on sale. It paid off as we got ringside seats to the show for a reasonable price (£30 each).

I remember Juventud Guerrera and Psicosis opening the show with a super cruiserweight match for the WWA International Cruiserweight Championship, another favourite of mine 'World's Most Dangerous Man' Ken Shamrock was advertised (he didn't appear) as was Jerry 'The King' Lawler (who also didn't appear).

I also remember the commentary happening live for everyone to hear (that was pretty cool), a Tables match between Crowbar and NXT trainer Norman Smiley which was pretty wild, Bret 'The Hitman' Hart was guest Referee as Jeff Jarrett (c) defended the WWA World Heavyweight title against 'Big Poppa Pump' Scott Steiner and Road Dogg – Jarrett cheated and Bret put him in the sharpshooter post-match to the delight of myself and the crowd.

I bought my first pro wrestling t-shirt 'Slapnutz', yeah I was a fan of 'The Chosen One' Jeff Jarrett. We were ringside (a few rows back) so when my favourite all-time professional wrestler Bret 'The Hitman' Hart came by, I passed my autograph book to my Brother, he passed it forward and when it was passed back, amazingly I had Bret's autograph – I was on cloud nine!

I would go on to meet Jake 'The Snake' Roberts and 'Hacksaw' Jim Duggan (Hooooooooooo! U-S-A, U-S-A!) at the N.E.C. which was pretty cool, but I was left a little disappointed that I couldn't meet Alex Shane who I had become a fan of because of Talksport.

4. 2002

FWA 'Revival' was shown on Bravo (a UK television channel) on Sunday 3rd March 2002 at 8pm. I remember sitting down unsure on what I was about to witness but really excited about it at the same time. FWA 'Revival' was a great show.

Watching 'Latino Heat' Eddie Guerrero vs Doug Williams was a wrestling purists dream and the aerial athleticism of 'The Phoenix' Jody Fleisch was there for all to see. Also on the card most notably were 'Wonderkid' Jonny Storm, Flash Barker, NXT Trainer Robby Brookside and 'Highlander from Hell' Drew McDonald.

From here I saw through magazine readings that Jonny Storm, Jody Fleisch and Doug Williams made their way over to America for Ring Of Honor – where they competed in ROH 'Road to the Title', Williams made it to the Final (60 Minute Four Way Iron Man Match) with 'Fallen Angel' Christopher Daniels, Low Ki and Spanky. Storm and Fleisch did great in Combat Zone Wrestling – Storm vs. Fleisch was an amazing match at CZW Best Of The Best 2.

British Wrestling had gone global!

FWA came back in to my focus with a stellar 'British Uprising' card on 13th October 2002... James Tighe vs Jack Xavier vs Raj Ghosh almost stole the show with a super opening match, Doug Williams vs Jerry Lynn put forth a technical wrestling masterpiece, Jonny Storm vs AJ Styles was superb and the main event between Flash Barker (c) and Jody Fleisch showed the lengths Fleisch would go to win the FWA British Heavyweight Title in a

Ladder Match – when he moonsaulted off of the balcony! A truly unbelievable moment.

5. 2003

The next time I came across British Wrestling was 'Frontiers of Honour' FWA/ROH which took place on 17th May 2003.

I remember reading glowing reviews and when I saw my favourite modern day wrestler Paul London was on the show I made the purchase. Paul London and James Tighe had a very good match which shone a brighter spotlight on Tighe, Burchill (a man I had only heard about) looked amazing as he destroyed two men.

Jonny Storm had a cracking match with the much talked about AJ Styles. Flash Barker really impressed me with his performance against Low Ki. Female Wrestler Nikita dived off of a balcony! Jody Fleisch vs Christopher Daniels was a really good main event, this was a top notch show.

This proved without a shadow of a doubt that British Wrestling could go toe to toe with its American counterparts.

6. 2004
THE WRESTLING CHANNEL

In March 2004 SKY TV Launched The Wrestling Channel. The best show ratings and content-wise had to be World of Sport. I was far too young to remember W.O.S. in its heyday but I remember people saying that it was incredibly popular and was a fixture of Saturday afternoon TV. Having not watched any of the first run coverage from the 1960's until 1988 (when it was cancelled). I was really looking forward to watching British Wrestling on TWC.

It was during this time that I saw just how amazing Johnny Saint, Dynamite Kid, Steve Grey, Les Kellet, Mark 'Rollerball' Rocco, Marty Jones, Jim Breaks and countless others were. I remember sitting there in awe during Johnny Saint vs Steve Grey, Dynamite Kid vs Mark 'Rollerball' Rocco and Marty Jones vs Owen Hart in particular. I know that World of Sport was popular with the masses because of Big Daddy and Giant Haystacks in particular but for me I was drawn to the Middleweights which the likes of above wrestlers (stated) were. I preferred technical expertise to a battle between two goliaths.

The Wrestling Channel was just amazing like I have said above, it showed just how great British Wrestling use to be via World of Sport. At the same time it showed just how good it was nowadays via the shows I have talked about previously ROH 'Road To The Title', CZW 'Best Of The Best 2' and FWA 'British Uprising' – I watched for the very first time on TWC. It is a real shame that The Wrestling

Channel is not around to this day as it was essential viewing.

Over the years I had read more and more negative viewpoints on professional wrestling which I didn't understand because if you love it, why would you seemingly hate it so much?

On 29th May 2004 (2 days before my 19th Birthday) my Brother surprised me with a Ticket to a WWE RAW House Show in my hometown (Birmingham, England). After watching Ric Flair vs Shawn Michaels, Batista vs Edge and Shelton Benjamin vs Randy Orton (c) for WWE Intercontinental Title in particular I decided that I would share my (a regular Fan's) perspective with the world.

Batista vs Edge was the opening match and it did a great job of warming up the crowd for the show ahead. Benjamin vs Orton was a really well worked athletic contest with the twist of the I.C. Title 'changing' hands before the match was re-started.

Flair vs Michaels was just incredible, really quick paced, counters and reversals, bell to bell action - this match in particular made me want to write. Seeing Legends Ric Flair and Shawn Michaels go all out for 30 minutes at a House Show (not taped for TV) made me want to write and tell the world all about it.

I started writing as soon as I returned from the show and I have loved doing so ever since.

During the summer of 2004 Doug Williams won a Tournament to capture the Vacant ROH Pure Title, this just goes to show how respected British Wrestling was becoming once more, as Williams was a proponent of World Of Sport style wrestling and his holding of a major U.S. Championship was definitely a feather in the cap for British Wrestling.

7. 2005
THE YEAR OF THE SUPERSHOWS

With the early success of The Wrestling Channel it was announced that on 19th March 2005 a Supershow called TWC International Showdown would be held in Coventry, England at the Coventry Skydome.

Even though I was living in Bolton, England (where I was studying at the time) there was no way I was missing this show! Especially after seeing the announced matches, Samoa Joe vs CM Punk and a TNA X Division title match between AJ Styles and Christopher Daniels (c) in particular caught my eye.

I came back so I could go to the meet and greet, I met 'Phenomenal' AJ Styles, Samoa Joe, 'Wonderkid' Jonny Storm, fellow Brummie Spud, Raven, and the man who was an inspiration to continue the lifestyle I am living (not drinking, smoking, taking drugs), which I would find out meant 'straightedge' – CM Punk.

I had brief chats with each and bought two Ring of Honor t-shirts, Bryan Danielson 'I will break you' and CM Punk's 'Straightedge' t-shirt. I left the meet and greet and met up with my Brother to go to the show.

Highlights included: Chris Sabin vs Jonny Storm vs Spud vs Petey Williams – this was a great way to start the show, my first time seeing fellow Brummie Spud and he didn't seem overawed by being in the ring with Storm, Sabin or Williams which is a testament to him. Samoa Joe vs CM Punk was a superb match and a great addition to their ROH rivalry.

Mitsuharu Misawa/Yoshinari Ogawa/Tiger Emperor vs Doug Williams/Scorpio/James Tighe - another really good match where Emperor and Tighe looked really good with their more experienced partners and opponents.

TNA X-Division title match: AJ Styles vs Christopher Daniels (c) - was a sensational match and a fitting main event to end a top notch show. My Brother wanted to get away because of traffic but I made sure we stayed behind to watch the two shake hands because I was so enthralled.

With British wrestling on the rise in mid-2005 I heard about a new promotion that was making waves, 'One Pro Wrestling' - they were advertising an All-star card of wrestling/wrestlers from around the world.

The one name that drew attention to the promotion was Matt Hardy. Hardy was a fan favourite who had received a raw deal in WWE and because of this he was the hottest free agent in professional wrestling.

1PW made the deal to sign Hardy up and titled their first show 'Twist of Fate' – Hardy dropped out to re-sign with WWE so the show was renamed 'A Cruel Twist of Fate'. The show split critics down the middle, most wanted 1PW to fail (other promoters mainly), the fans wanted the show to succeed because they were getting their money's worth and then some. This turned into an Us vs Them mentality between 1PW and other companies in the UK.

In amongst all of this was the announcement that another Supershow called Universal Uproar would happen in Coventry at Coventry Skydome on 12th November 2005. This was shaping up to be a great card with a salivating contest between AJ Styles and Austin Aries pencilled in.

Unfortunately the 'card subject to change' tag was ever present in the build up to the show. TNA Wrestling had a PPV the very next day and stopped their talent from performing on the show. This was a really big shame. With that being said Alex Shane did his very best to put on a show worthy of the 'Supershow' title.

Regardless I booked mine & my Brother's ticket and luckily I had a mate (Alex) at University who gave me a lift back (most of the way) as he was travelling through on his way to Norwich. I promised I would get him Mick Foley's autograph, as he was a big fan.

I made my way once more to the meet and greet – I met the legendary Bill Apter who I asked, "What is your favourite pro wrestling match?"

He replied "The Ric Flair vs Ricky Steamboat series of matches."

I met D'lo Brown who I had been a fan of since WWE days, Joe Legend, Shannon Moore, Stevie Knight, Homicide, Low Ki (who almost broke my hand with a handshake!), James Tighe, Doug Williams, Japanese star Jun Akiyama, Simply Luscious, Nigel McGuinness who allowed me to hold ROH Pure Wrestling Title (which was pretty cool).

I met Spud again and complimented him on four way showing from TWC international showdown (months earlier) and I did meet Mick Foley – who I got an autograph for Alex from, it was just disappointing that it seemed Foley was more interested in the money than making a fan happy.

I met up with my Brother and we took our seats closer to the ring this time. This would cause problems with people standing, etc.

Highlights included: a fast paced opening match featuring five of the top cruiserweights in the UK ('Wonderkid' Jonny Storm, Jody Fleisch, Spud, James Tighe and Aviv Maayan) and worldwide sensation The Amazing Red. Colt Cabana vs Nigel McGuinness (World of Sport) match was what the TWC International Showdown needed to be – fantastic.

Around half way through McGuinness vs Cabana we made the decision to move so we went up to the bleachers (where we sat for TWC International Showdown) and weirdly had a much better view. Since this day I have always been a tiered seat over ringside seat fan.

Low Ki vs Homicide was a sensational match! Doug Williams & Jun Akiyama vs Go Shiozaki & Kenta Kobashi was the Pro Wrestling NOAH style main event everyone was expecting, it was amazing seeing Kobashi live and feeling the aura of the man.

I met up with Alex and he was chuffed with me getting Mick Foley's autograph for him, not so much with the reason behind it. Not long after arriving back in Bolton I was met with the unfortunate news of one of my favourite wrestlers, 'Latino Heat' Eddie Guerrero, passing away. I had gone from the ultimate high to a very deep low in the space of 24 hours.

From here I found out about Myspace (it was popular at the time!) and I found information that a lot of the wrestlers were now all attainable to talk to online (which was mind blowing at the time), I signed up for Myspace and used it as my tool to connect with those in the wrestling business and beyond.

Towards the end of my time on Myspace I had reached over 10,000+ blog and profile views.

8. 2006

Around this time I met another friend from University, Elmar, and after finding out he was a professional wrestling fan and lived near the area (Rotherham), with his brother Shaz's help we personally took in One Pro Wrestling for the first time in March 2006.

1PW 'All or Nothing' Night 1 and especially Night 2 were tremendous and well worth the money we paid to see them.

Night 1 - Christopher Daniels vs Jerry Lynn, Samoa Joe vs Austin Aries and AJ Styles vs Samoa Joe in particular were superb matches.

Night 2 (one of the best shows I have ever watched Live or on DVD) – Christopher Daniels vs Austin Aries, AJ Styles vs Jerry Lynn, Scorpio vs Sterling James Keenan (relatively unknown at the time – now known as Commentator Corey Graves on WWE RAW/NXT), Jody Fleisch & Jonny Storm vs The Rottweilers (Homicide & Ricky Reyes) and AJ Styles vs Christopher Daniels vs Samoa Joe (c) for the TNA X Division Title were all really good or great.

It was also during this time, although I was super nervous with Elmar's support that I met 'Fallen Angel' Christopher Daniels who I was able to give a piece of my work to.

"Hi Chris, I just wanted to give you a piece of my work."

He replied, "Thank You," and took it in his hand, something for the plane ride home. This was a personal highlight of mine.

During early 2006 it was announced that Ring of Honor would be bringing their show to the UK (in Liverpool and Broxbourne respectively).

Although I had left Bolton in May, I made the trip back up north and with the help of another University friend Pete, I was able to go to ROH 'Unified' as I was able to stay at his house.

We arrived at Liverpool Olympia, where the ROH Fanslam was taking place at 12:30pm. Cary Silkin was waiting outside, greeting fans. After 5 minutes of chatting with fans in the queue, the fans chanted "ROH! ROH! ROH!" this was taped for the release of this show on DVD. We entered ROH Fanslam and met a couple of fans by the name of Chud and Jamie who stated to be my non wrestling friend, "This show will be awesome!"

From a British Wrestling point of view we were well represented. 'Wonderkid' Jonny Storm and Spud were a part of a super opening match...

4 Corner Survival

Colt Cabana vs 'Wonderkid' Jonny Storm vs Spud vs Matt Sydal

4 Corner Survival Rules:
Two wrestlers start the match. Tags can be made at any point. Once a wrestler leaves the ring another one can enter without being tagged. The match ends by a pinfall or submission.

A good match to kick off ROH's Debut show in Liverpool, England on their first UK Tour. This match had elements of comedy in it as Colt Cabana was trying to and successfully entertained the crowd.

Making him a clear Fan Favourite as chants of, "Colt Cabana, Colt Cabana!" sounded throughout the Olympia. With Spud down on the mat, Sydal ascended the turnbuckle and hit his finishing move, the Sydal Star Press, for the 1, 2, 3.

Winner: Matt Sydal

ROH World Tag Titles #1 Contendership

Doug Williams & Jody Flesich vs Team NOAH
(Suwa and Go Shiozaki)

A good match, featuring some good old school tag team wrestling with back and forth action. The match ended when Williams reversed Shiozaki's attempt at a roll up and hit his Finishing move the Chaos Theory for the 1, 2, 3.

This could have been Match of the Night if not for a couple of classics later in the card.

Winners and NEW #1 Contenders for ROH World Tag Team Titles: Doug Williams & Jody Fleisch

Post-Match:
Suwa attacks Shiozaki with his kendo stick until Williams and Fleisch intervene and the fans show appreciation to the three men.

FWA Title Chad Collyer vs Robby Brookside (c)

Robby Brookside (FWA Champion at the time) was a part of a solid match with Chad Collyer.

Although a slow starter, a match the fans found difficult to get into due to its methodical pace. The action began to pick up, as there were a series of reversals and some good technical wrestling.

The end of the match happened when Brookside hit a Cross-Arm Bomb while Collyer was sitting on the top rope and followed it up with a roll through pin for the 1, 2, 3.

Winner and STILL FWA Champion: Robby Brookside (c)

ROH World Title merging with ROH Pure Title
Bryan Danielson vs Nigel McGuinness

Although Nigel McGuinness made his name in America, he is also British and he was involved in an incredible main event against 'The Best Wrestler in the World' Bryan Danielson.

Rules for tonight's ROH World/ROH Pure Title Unification match:
The match will take place under ROH Pure Title rules, meaning you have three rope breaks during the match. The Titles can change hands on disqualification (DQ), count-out, pinfall and submission. The match will have no time limit. In the event of a double DQ, or double count-out, the match will be restarted as there will be a Winner and a New Unified ROH World Champion.

Back-Story:

Bryan Danielson is arguably the best wrestler in the World, having defeated James Gibson at Glory By Honor 4 for ROH World Title (17th September 2005). Danielson has taken on and beaten all comers, except Challenger Nigel McGuinness who defeated him by count-out on April 29th 2006 (at ROH Night of Champions Night 2).

Danielson has since cancelled out that victory with a win on July 29th 2006. McGuinness has held the ROH Pure Title since beating Samoa Joe at ROH Dragon Gate Invasion (27th August 2005). Making McGuinness the longest reigning Champion in ROH since 2005. McGuinness has beaten everyone that has been placed in front of him, including ROH World Champion Bryan Danielson.

So with wins between the two (tied at 1-1) this is the rubber match. The stakes have been raised, now this is one of the most important matches in ROH History, because with no Title changes in ROH since 2005 there will finally be one in this match, as the ROH Titles (World and Pure) are being merged together tonight.

Match:
This was a truly great and at times gripping match which encapsulated everything that is great about Ring of Honor. Bryan Danielson and Nigel McGuinness put on a clinic of technical wrestling expertise before it turned into a fight. After the rope breaks were used by both men the action spilled to the floor where Danielson promptly ran McGuinness's head into the ring post four times busting McGuinness wide open.

Upon returning to the ring McGuinness put up a valiant effort which seemed to anger Danielson, who came forth with a barrage of elbows and the referee had no choice but to stop the match and award the newly merged ROH World Title to Bryan Danielson.

Winner and NEW Unified ROH World Champion: Bryan Danielson (c)

Post-Match:
Bryan Danielson picks up the microphone: "Nigel, you act tough in front of all these idiots... but, that was the toughest match of my reign as ROH World Champion, how about we do this one more time in St. Paul, Minnesota on August 25th?"

McGuinness responds: "If you want it (points to the fans), you have got it." The two men shake hands and leave the ring.

Match of the Night:
ROH World Title merging with ROH Pure Title
Bryan Danielson vs Nigel McGuinness

The British Wrestling scene played a part in ROH 'Unified' success.

We had an interesting train ride back to Bolton, Super Oli! We got back to his and I was pretty pumped so I wrote my ROH Fanslam & ROH 'Unified' reports and I sent them to various internet websites.

1PW 1 Year Anniversary Show (14th October 2006)

Unfortunately I have misplaced my full 1PW reports, I only have the best of matches – that I have written below.

El Ligero vs El Generico

What a way to start a show! This was an insane match with fast paced Lucha style wrestling. Ligero doesn't look out of place in there with the more experienced Generico. Both wrestlers trade armdrags and other classic Lucha style manoeuvres. Ligero goes to Amazing Red's playbook and hits the Code Red for a close nearfall!

The contest keeps up it's fever pitch like style until Ligero hits a hurricanrana and then finishes off Generico with a C4L (Jumping DDT off the ropes) for the 1, 2 and 3. In what ended a very good opening match.

The two men shake hands after the match in a show of respect.

Winner: El Ligero

Video comes on the screen: Dustin Rhodes and Christopher Daniels have food poisoning!!! Loud booing can be heard.

"Coming to the ring from Hollywood, California, wait a second? It's Goldustin!!!" Oh my god! "He's hot, he's spicy, he tastes great. Curryman!!!" No way!

Goldustin vs Curryman

This was a very good match with a lot of comedy involved! Curryman dances with the Ref during an armlock. Fans are immersed in the action also with duel chants "Let's go Curryman/Let's go Goldust." Funny moment when Curryman and Goldustin try to stamp on each other's feet, they can't, so they both stamp on the Ref's feet!

More comedy moments, Goldustin kicks the Ref but this time the Ref kicks back! Match gets more serious as Curryman hits the STO and Best Ever Moonsault but Goldustin kicks out after a long 2 count. Finish comes when Goldustin hits the Curtain Call for the 1, 2, and 3!

Winner: Goldustin

PAC's Proving Match

AJ Styles vs PAC

The biggest match of PAC's career thus far! Handshake to start off. Match becomes a game of chess with both men seeking but not gaining the advantage that is until AJ hits his signature dropkick which knocks PAC for a loop. AJ takes control of the match and shows he can use submission moves in his arsenal also. PAC tries to up the pace and with this he takes control of the match, PAC shows his amazing athleticism with a Sky twister press from the top rope to AJ at ringside!

"This is awesome" chants start up. The last few minutes are frantic as both men look for that killer move to end the match. Dragon suplex attempt by PAC, AJ blocks. AJ then hits a lot of vicious knees to PAC's midsection and then nails the Styles-Clash for the 1, 2 and 3!

Winner: AJ Styles

El Ligero showed that he is a star in the making. Goldustin vs Curryman was all kinds of fun! AJ vs PAC was the show stealer everyone thought it would be and although it is overused, a sure fire Match of the Year candidate!

TBW 'Overload' (20th October 2006)

Not long after returning from 1PW, I was contacted by promoter Jamie Worthing about helping with the lighting for Total Brutality Wrestling. The locality of the promotion made it a viable option, so I made the trip. It was on this show TBW 'Overload' that I met Joel Redman (he became Oliver Grey in WWE NXT) straight away I saw star potential.

I also met The Heartbreak Express (Phil and Sean Davis) they are pretty good guys and I enjoyed their match. Match of the Night honours went to El Ligero vs British Born Steele – they had a good solid match.

The Lighting went off without a hitch and being placed in The Balcony meant I had the best seat in the house, so I was pretty happy. I also got paid for helping out and put up in a hotel as well, so I really enjoyed my TBW experience.

Leicester Pro Wrestling (November/December 2006)

After my experience with TBW, I was in contact with LPW who were running shows local to me. I turned up wanting to write about the show but on one occasion the Ring Announcer didn't show up so I was asked if I would like to do it, I did.

Although I was told my announcing was 'very American' giving kids in the audience my autograph after the show was an amazing experience. From here I worked as part of a commentary team, which was pretty cool apart from the one night when we forgot to turn my microphone on, oops!

9. 2007
TAKING A CLOSER LOOK AT BRITISH WRESTLING

A little background first, I heard about Anti Watershed Wrestling/Alternative Wrestling World (AWW) first of all because of a highlight video I saw on Youtube advertising PAC (WWE's Neville) and after seeing him perform at 1PW months before I was like wow, impressive. I then found out that AWW ran in my hometown of Birmingham, England and decided to make the decision that I would take a closer look at the British wrestling scene.

January 2007

Anti-Watershed Wrestling

LATZ addressed BBS and AWW management: A few audio difficulties made this hard to hear but LATZ basically called out BBS!

British Born Steele vs Latz

BBS of course obliges and with that a good opening match takes place. BBS is one of rising stars on the British independents (having a very good match vs El Ligero back in TBW in October), Latz I have not seen before, but he also looked very capable on this night. After around 10 minutes of back and forth action, BBS defeated Latz with the exact move that got him the victory in the last show, a sunset powerbomb from the top turnbuckle.

Ronin vs 'Star Man' Mark Clarke

This was a hard hitting short match, Clarke was steamrolled by the bigger man Ronin, having little to no offense. Ronin looked impressive on this first outing for AWW. That wasn't enough for Ronin though as he attacked the defenceless Clarke after the bell with his version of the splash, adding insult to injury!

Nick Knight unable to appear – Desirable Danny D addresses the situation: The scheduled match between Nick Knight and Geraden was forced to be cancelled as Nick Knight did not want to "Leave the luxury surroundings of his home city, Worcester to come to the 'gutter' known as Digbeth."

Desirable Danny D announced that he was still intent on putting Geraden in his place and had another opponent for him. This was announced as Mad Man Manson.

Mad Man Manson vs Geraden

Mad Man Manson is just that, absolutely mad! Personally he is becoming a favourite wrestler of mine, he can wrestle and damn he is entertaining. Crazy match, where the Ref was being wrestled and all sorts of comedic antics!

Geraden must have wished he stayed at home. Good comedy match, Geraden tried to compete with

Manson but Manson's craziness was just too much.
Manson wins with his sit-down slam.

Metal Militia (Axel Adams & Pure Xtasy) vs Tommy Gunn & Weasel

The Militia start the match off by attacking Gunn and Weasel from behind! Metal Militia looked impressive, by singling out Weasel for most of the match, while Gunn was chomping at the bit to get in the ring.

Finally Weasel made the tag, Gunn came in all guns blazing, but was shot down after a short rally and hit with a Doomsday Device by the Militia for the 1, 2, 3!

Lord Graham Thomas vs A.J. Kid Irish

Match had an old school vs new school feel, with Graham using old school moves like a wristlock, while AJ was trying to use his quickness and agility to out manoeuvre his opponent. Graham tried every trick in the book, but could not get the better of the young up and comer. Graham finally managed to outwit AJ when he pushed powder in his and the Ref's eyes, but just as victory looked a formality... The man called GBH, returns!!

GBH entered the ring and completely wiped out Lord Graham Thomas. GBH then raised the arm of AJ but then nailed home his second shocker of the night by taking him out too! GBH gave AJ a severe beating and put the exclamation point with two devastating chokeslams.

Carnage vs 'The Slaphead Superman' Keego Ward

The match I personally paid £5 ticket price to see Keego Ward's AWW debut, and seconds later the fans are covered by sprayed water, way to a dear yourself to the crowd Keego! Carnage entered the ring to much fanfare, as he has been a fan favourite after revered performances in 2006 for AWW. This was the first pure wrestling match on the card, with both men trading holds and reversals during the early going.

Keego began to grow frustrated at his inability to put away Carnage, and started using unhanded tactics. Carnage was not phased by this though, as he has been known to use such unhanded tactics himself! Keego couldn't outwit Carnage and his AWW debut ended in defeat after Carnage hit the devastating 'Carnage-Bolt' for the 1, 2, 3.

Hardcore Rules

Johnny Lee vs Dan Ryder

Well that was my £5 well spent time to go home! Well not quite, there was still a main event to go. How to become stars in one night? Give the fans everything you have for the sake of their entertainment!

I'm not sure how I can do this match justice, but wow it was incredible! The match started out much like the previous match with both men battling for the pinfall, with short and quick pinfall attempts, during this exchange Ryder gets tied up in the ropes, oh it is a Hardcore match. From this moment the match turned into a full out war!

Lee attacked Ryder with everything from a Cookie Sheet to a Steel Chair taking the action around the ringside area. Ryder took a vicious beating (at one point) being swung headfirst into the ringpost! The thud from that echoed around the building! Ryder somehow came back into the contest and had Lee on the back foot, until he tried a piledriver, this was reversed into a back body drop on the floor!

The match continues to get bloodier and more gruesome, Ryder tries in vain to make yet another comeback, but that ringpost shot earlier in the match has him punch drunk. Lee sees this and takes Ryder to the entrance stage, from here he sets up a piledriver (at least that is what the fans think!).

Lee jumps with Ryder in the Canadian Destroyer off the Entrance ramp through a Table! This has to be seen to be believed! The match gracefully ends, with the fans going crazy as the pinfall takes place.

I paid my £5 to see Carnage vs Keego Ward, but for that £5 I got see Madman Manson entertain like only he can, up and comer BBS and two relative unknowns (Dan Ryder vs Johnny Lee) take my Match of The Year for 2007 thus far!

A few days later I left my job as a Wine Waiter at The Hilton Birmingham Metropole, after searching and searching for a new job in the coming months (nothing to be found). So I continued attending shows...

All Star Wrestling

Date: 14th February 2007
Location: Leamington Spa, England
Attendance: Sold Out (400)

ASW has a stellar reputation for putting on fun family friendly shows, with Leamington Spa not being a million miles away, I decided to make the trip. The opening match between ASW British Mid Heavyweight Champion Dean Allmark (c) and Robbie Dynamite made it all worthwhile! This was a cracking way to start the show and I became a fan of both wrestlers immediately.

This was my first time seeing Nick Aldis (AKA Magnus) and although he was fairly new (second year wrestling) you could see he had potential. Jetta vs Lisa Fury was a fun women's match, it was great seeing Gangrel live and I enjoyed his match against British Veteran James Mason.

The main event with The Liverpool Lads (NXT Trainer Robby Brookside & Frankie Sloan) vs Broady Steele & Joe Legend was a good way to cap the evening's entertainment - England vs USA always makes for fine viewing.

I thoroughly enjoyed my night out watching All Star Wrestling and I highly recommend it to anyone who likes a family oriented product.

ROH Doubleshot (March 3rd & 4th 2007 from Liverpool Olympia, Liverpool, England)

In late 2006 as I was posting on ROH Forums, I began talking with a guy called Austin Howell. We began to make plans for him to come over to England for the ROH Shows – where we could go to both shows and he could stay at mine after.

The hotel we stayed at much to our amazement was the same as the ROH Crew. ROH Ring Announcer Bobby Cruise who I recently interviewed was there and even though I was stupidly tired, Austin persuaded me to go and meet him.

It was good meeting him in person after spending a lot of time putting together an interview, promoting the shows. We also talked at length with Mark & Jay – The Briscoes. I tried unsuccessfully to help with an adapter for a computer console in Julius Smoke's room. We went out for dinner with the guys and girls, I got chopped by Roderick Strong – it hurts. I got on really well with BJ Whitmer after I said I was a fan of his match vs Homicide (ROH Main Event Spectacles '03).

We said our goodbyes and headed off to bed, Austin and myself chatted into the night, not believing our good luck!

The next day I helped Mark & Jay with the exchange rates when they were buying breakfast. Then we were given the news that Alex Shane had overbooked the coach and Mark, Jay, Sara Del Rey & Alison Danger needed to get to Liverpool another way. I stepped up and said I can help – Me and Austin were getting the train, they could just join us.

We helped with Alison's and Sara's luggage - being the gentlemen we are and headed to Liverpool. We got there with no concerns and after transferring over to a Taxi whilst in Liverpool, we were soon at the Olympia. Alex Shane thanked me and we helped put up the ring and then just chilled before the show.

Unlike the previous August where the UK contingent were all prevalent on ROH 'Unified' on this occasion only Nigel McGuinness, PAC, Eden Black and Jetta were on the cards.

Night 1 – PAC tore it up with Roderick Strong (c) for the Full Impact Pro Heavyweight Championship, Eden Black & Jetta cut a promo where they hyped a match to take place on Night 2 and Nigel McGuinness gave departing Samoa Joe a heck of main event match to cap the night's show.

On the way back I shared pictures with BJ Whitmer but in doing so really annoyed Alison Danger and she tore into me when we got off the coach.

I was taken aback about this and chatted into the night with Austin about it. Fortunately the next day – Sara Del Rey (NXT Trainer Sara Amato) was so sweet that she made me feel better about the previous evening. We ended up having breakfast with Julius Smoke & Homicide, I got talking to Smokes about an interview and felt even better (it didn't come to pass unfortunately).

Night 2 – Eden Black & Jetta took on Sara Del Rey & Alison Danger (Dangerous Angels) they did the best that they could for the lack of time they were given (less than 7 minutes), Matt Sydal and PAC had a super-fast paced blink and you might miss it match and Nigel McGuinness vs Jimmy Rave (Fight Without Honor) was a fitting conclusion to a truly brutal feud with a fantastic match to cap it all.

A friend I had met through 1PW (Steve) was able to meet Samoa Joe after his last night in ROH (at the time), which was a huge thrill for him and Dan (who I had met at LPW), myself and Austin went back to the hotel. Austin stayed at mine for a couple of days before meeting up with Alison Danger in London – I did try and apologize for annoying her, via an email with photos of Eden Black & Jetta vs Herself & Sara Del Rey, she didn't respond.

Although less British Wrestlers were used on these shows it was still great to see they could compete with the rest of the world.

Working for the Greater Good – A Charity Show

After watching a match between up and comer Ashton Smith and British Wrestling Veteran Keith Myatt (good match with a great storytelling) at LPW. I was approached to go to and cover a Charity Show by Keith Myatt (one of the nicest guys in the business), I said if I can be there, I would be. From here I was put in contact with British Born Steele and after meeting with him & Ashton Smith we made the drive up to Stoke-On-Trent.

The wrestlers foregoed their fees to wrestle on the show and I got to witness Myatt team with his trainer 'Wildman' John Wilkie take on the team of British Born Steele and Ashton – a tremendous story of veterans vs underdogs was told, Hubba Bubba Lucha exploded as El Ligero took on Bubblegum in the Match of the Night.

I also was able to see another top notch match between Myatt and Ashton (who were wrestling for the second time on this evening).

The show raised a good amount of money for Charity and it was really refreshing to see everyone work together for the greater good in professional wrestling.

10. THE RETURN

I sat down with my Mom and stated, "Nothing is happening on the job front Mom, I really love writing about professional wrestling, I think I can make a go of it, if I travel around the UK reporting on shows."

Mom replied, "If that is what you want to do, you should still look for (normal) work but I will support you in any way I can."

With my Mom's backing I returned to the British Wrestling scene in September 2007.

SEPTEMBER 2007

Wrestling Association of Rugby – W.A.R. Buried Alive

Date: Saturday 8th September 2007
Time: 7:30pm
Attendance: Near capacity a few empty seats.
Price: Adults: £5, Under 15's: £4
Location: Lawrence Sheriff Grammar School, Clifton Road, Rugby.

Grudge Match

Nero vs Fireman Stan

Fans boo loudly as Nero enters and chant, "You suck!" The fans cheer loudly as Fireman Stan enters. Stan dresses the Ref up like a Fireman, Nero sneaks in from behind and rolls him up (believing he is Stan) and Stan counts to two before the Ref kicks out! Nero

and Stan crisscross the ropes and Stan slides out of
the ring, hilariously Nero keeps running. Stan re-
enters the ring and points up (Nero looks up) so Stan
slaps him across the face.

Nero tries to repay the favour but is slapped once
again. Fans chant "Stan, Stan, Stan!" Nero elbows
Stan as he attempts a corner splash and follows that
up with a vicious dropkick to Stan's knee. Stan looks
injured!? Stan is helped to the back by the Referees
as he is unable to continue. Nero attacks Stan from
behind and brings him back to the ring. Nero applies
the spinning toe hold on Stan but Stan will not quit,
Stan in desperation manages to hit a spinebuster and
both men are down.

The ref starts the count 1, 2, 3, 4, 5, 6, 7 and both
men are to their feet once more, Nero hits the
incoming Stan with a double boot followed by a
dropkick. Then he heads up the turnbuckle for a
moonsault… Stan is able to move out of the way,
Nero runs at Stan, Stan hits the Fireman Slam for the
1, 2 and 3!

Winner: Fireman Stan

The Executioner & Red Tiger enter the ring, the
Executioner attacks Stan. Fans direct, "You suck!"
chants at Tiger, Executioner hits his finishing move
the Chokebomb on Stan. He then takes the
microphone. "Shut the hell up," he tells the fans.
"I've never been pinned, no man can beat me!" Tiger
opens the casket and W.A.R. Heavyweight Champion
Louie Zerr (c) comes out and attacks the Executioner.
Fans chant "Louie, Louie!" Louie takes the

microphone; "I don't have to pin you! I've got to shove you in that casket and shut the lid."

Dante w/Roselyn vs Wheeler

The Ref takes Dante's Singapore cane away, Wheeler seeing his opportunity hits a step-up enziguri. Dante retreats, Wheeler follows so Dante uses Roselyn as a shield and then sucker punches Wheeler (the fans boo loudly). Drop toe hold by Wheeler gets a two count, Roselyn gets up on the apron and distracts Wheeler, who walks right into a Sky High by Dante for a close nearfall. Dante shows his sinister side by choking Wheeler when the Ref isn't looking.

Back suplex by Dante on Wheeler, Dante picks him up and executes another but as he attempts a third Wheeler manages to reverse it into a bulldog. Both men are down the ref starts the count 1, 2, 3, 4, 5, 6!

Wheeler comes back once more with clotheslines, a flying head scissors and a chin breaker in quick succession, once again Roselyn distracts Wheeler this time to no effect as Wheeler nails Dante with a code red for a long two count. Wheeler climbs the turnbuckle, Roselyn distracts Wheeler yet again. Dante is able to crotch Wheeler and quickly follows up with a Tower of London for the 3 count. Wheeler leaves with applause ringing in his ears.

Winner: Dante w/Roselyn

B52 Lance Corporal vs Jimmy Ocean

Ring announcer announces Corporal as, "The man that puts the fun in confrontational." Ref checks both men for illegal objects. "Jimmy, Jimmy!" chants by the fans. Corporal offers Jimmy a handshake (Jimmy looks for the crowds approval) and then shakes Corporal's hand, and gets sucker punched for his naivety. Ocean fires back with a series of forearms and a dropkick sending Corporal to the outside. High cross body by Ocean he then attempts to ram Corporal into the ringpost (Corporal blocks), so does Ocean, Corporal goes shoulder first into the ringpost.

Ocean attempts another high cross body this time Corporal blocks and rams Ocean back first into the ringpost. Fans chant "Jimmy" in unison. Ocean attempts a super kick Corporal reverses into a knee to the stomach for a two count, Corporal frustrated by his inability to put Ocean away starts using some underhand tactics unbeknownst to the Referee. Ocean is locked in a bearhug the Referee raises his hand it drops twice but on the third time, Ocean rakes Corporal's eyes and lands a DDT.

"Jimmy, Jimmy!" chants once more, Ocean follows that with a head scissors and boot into a hurricanrana on Corporal which sends him to the outside once more. Ocean soon follows with a slingshot press to the floor. Ocean attempts the superkick once more and again it is countered this time into a full nelson slam by Corporal. Corporal attempts a suplex from inside to outside of the ring Ocean manages to fend him off and runs towards the opposite ropes and sunset flip power bombs Corporal on the wooden floor!

Ref leads a count 1, 2, 3, 4, 5, 6, 7! Both men return to the ring. Ocean goes up to the top rope for an axe handle Corporal counters that into his AA spine buster for the 1, 2 and 3. Fans clap loudly as Ocean exits the ring.

Winner: B52 Lance Corporal

Four Man Ladder match for #1 Contendership to W.A.R. Heavyweight Title

'Old School' Dan London vs 'King Of Spin' Spindoctor vs Tank vs 'Bird Of Prey' Falcon

Tank and London shake hands as do Spindoctor and Falcon. All four men exit the ring straight away in search of a ladder. Spindoctor's ladder catapult hits both London and Tank directly in the face, Falcon hits Tank with a monkey flip into the ladder. Falcon climbs the ladder but is shook off by London, flapjack on Spindoctor looks like it has dented the ring! Double flapjack on Falcon by London and Tank in exactly the same place (may not help matters).

Falcon is thrown head first into a ladder, London attempts to do the same thing again (this time Falcon slides out of the ring) Spindoctor hits London and Tank with a top rope double dropkick. Van Terminator by Falcon into the ladder into London's face, Falcon ascends the ladder but is shoulder blocked off by Tank. Spindoctor sets up a second ladder (all four men climb) and all four men fall just as quickly.

"Ginger Ninja" chants by the fans directed at Falcon.

Falcon and Tank climb, Tank is pushed off by Falcon who is inches away from the W.A.R. Heavyweight Title shot contract, Falcon has other ideas though and proceeds with a Swanton bomb from the top of the ladder onto Tank below! Spindoctor climbs the ladder but is caught by London's low blow and Spindoctor is then suplexed off the ladder.

Falcon, London and Spindoctor climb the two ladders, London and Spindoctor's ladder is shook by Falcon and they fall off into Tank leaving Falcon with his best chance to win the match, he takes it by pulling down the W.A.R. Heavyweight #1 Contenders contract to win the match.

Winner and NEW #1 Contender: 'Bird Of Prey' Falcon

INTERMISSION

Martial Arts Exhibition

Array of kicks by Danny to a club, then he breaks a board with his fist. Dante and The Judge interrupt the exhibition. Judge bellows, "I'm not impressed" and then attempts to break the wooden board (but fails). He then challenges Danny to a one on one match, which Danny accepts.

Danny vs Judge

Judge outwrestles Danny in the early going, Danny is able to recover and kicks Judge directly in the ass. Judge frustrated illegally chokes Danny behind the

Refs back, the fans start chanting, "Jelly belly!" at the Judge. Judge has too much strength for Danny as shown by an avalanche splash in the corner followed by a running cannonball on the fallen Danny. Judge takes Danny to the top rope and hits a fall away slam for a close nearfall.

Judge powerbombs Danny hard to the canvas but as the pinfall is taking place he pulls him up. Judge takes the microphone. "You could have taken the easy way out, now you are going to be punished!" Judge sets up another power bomb but Danny rolls through 1, 2 and 3! The fans go crazy for Danny!!

Winner: Danny

Red Tiger's Cruiserweight Open Challenge

Red Tiger and Nero make their way to the ring. "Rob Hunter isn't here tonight, so I issue an open challenge."

'Mean Machine' Iggy Taylor answers the challenge. "Tonight you're going down, right here in Rugby."

Red Tiger vs Iggy Taylor

Iggy hits Tiger with a side effect and a bulldog for a two count. Iggy attempts a moonsault but Tiger moves (Iggy is able to land on his feet), this isn't advantageous though because he is quickly hit by a running boot. Tiger chokes Iggy in the corner (the fans boo loudly). Iggy rallies with a jumping hurricanrana and wheelbarrow into a DDT. Tiger retreats to ringside, Iggy attempts a suicide dive but is caught and thrown over head with a belly to belly suplex.

Tiger taunts the crowd. "The more you speak, the more he gets hurt." The action returns to the ring, Iggy manages to hit the code red for a close nearfall. Nero attacks Iggy from behind, Tiger heads up to the top rope (but he's wasting time taunting the crowd) Iggy crotches him on the turnbuckle and then hits a top rope twist of fate! Both men are down as the Ref starts the count 1, 2, 3, 4, 5, 6, 7, 8! Double jump whisper in the wind by Iggy, Tiger exits the ring. Asai moonsault by Iggy on Tiger and Nero, Nero distracts Iggy which leads to a hook DDT by Tiger (luckily for him Iggy's foot is under the ropes). Iggy attempts a twist of fate it's reversed into a splash mountain for the 1, 2 and 3!

Winner: Red Tiger

Casket Match for W.A.R. heavyweight Title

The Executioner vs Louie Zerr (c)

Fans chant, "You suck!" toward the Executioner, the fans surround Louie as he makes his way to the ring. Louie hits Executioner with a dropkick. Executioner lands in the casket. Louie tries to shut the lid but Executioner manages to escape. Kick and axe handle to the back by Executioner "Shut up, this could be you, kid." Executioner drags Louie out of the ring and hits a slam on the hard wooden floor, Executioner picks up Louie and suplexes him into the casket.

"Louie!" chants around the building, Louie is somehow able to escape. Back in the ring Louie attempts a high cross body but Executioner ducks out of the way, Executioner rolls Louie to outside. He picks Louie up and straddles him on side of the casket and follows that up with a big boot which knocks Louie into the casket. Executioner continues the attack and inadvertently knocks Louie outside the casket.

A ladder is brought into play, cross body off the ladder onto Executioner puts Louie in control. Louie forces Executioner into the casket Louie then dropkicks the lid but Executioner manages to escape. A chair is brought into play Executioner smacks Louie with it across the head he attempts a second shot but Louie dropkicks the chair into Executioner's face! Executioner is able to recover though, choke slamming Louie from the ring into the casket, he then shuts the lid and the match is over!

Executioner is the NEW W.A.R. Heavyweight Champion, Tiger congratulates him. "No man can beat me," cue #1 contender Falcon who appears the two men stare each other down as the show comes to a close.

Winner and NEW W.A.R. Heavyweight Champion: The Executioner (c)

A decent show which was highlighted by a thrilling ladder match that was worth the price of admission alone, the show had the right mix of entertainment and wrestling which sent the fans home happy.

Triple X Wrestling

Date: Sunday 9th September 2007
Time: 4pm
Attendance: Near capacity a few empty seats.
Price: £7
Location: Jumping Jaks, Coventry Skydome, Coventry.

Gabriel Grey makes his way to the ring, he is the host for the night's proceedings.

'Rockstar' Spud vs Devilman

Fans boo loudly as Spud enters the ring. Spud takes the microphone "My name is Spud, I'm here for rock and roll!" He continues, "Devilman represents each and every one of you."

Devilman enters the ring (the fans cheer loudly) and start a "Devil-man!" chant, the fans continue to taunt Spud with chants of, "Midget."

Spud retorts, "I'm not a midget, I'm just a very small man!" Devilman attempts a lock-up with Spud but Spud ducks and hits Devilman with two kicks to the leg. Another kick by Spud this time Devilman is unfazed and returns with a lariat, uppercut, suplex and front suplex in quick succession for a two count.

Spud rakes Devilman's eyes and follows that up with a dropkick to the knee, Spud then focuses his attack on Devilman's leg with a chop block, leg breaker and a leg snap. Spud poses for the crowd, fans chant "Devil-man" once more. Spud kicks Devilman in the back, Devilman returns the favour with two vicious kicks to Spud's back. Devilman's momentum is almost derailed when Spud hits the code red for a close nearfall, but Devilman rallies with a hurricane DDT for the 1, 2 and 3.

Winner: Devilman

Icons of Dominance (Scott Grimm & John Bull w/The Boss) vs CK Light & 'That 70's' Andy Shoes

Gabriel Grey announces that I.O.D. weigh in at 1300 buckets of KFC which elicits laughter from the crowd. Grimm and Bull attack Light and Shoes before the bell, Bull & Grimm double team Shoes after dumping Light to the outside.

"Shoes!" chant starts up, the Ref is distracted by Light allowing I.O.D. to double team Shoes further. Finally Shoes tags in Light who has a barrage of forearms for the I.O.D. he then attempts to take Bull off his feet (to no avail), Bull hits a knee to the face followed by a suplex to down Light. Light attempts a tag but Shoes isn't close enough I.O.D. hit a side slam and leg drop combination on Light for a two count.

Bull taunts Shoes who retorts with, "You big fat man!" which the fans pick up on starting a "Big-fat-man!" chant. Light struggles once more for the tag but is caught in a bearhug by Bull, Grimm distracts the Ref who doesn't see the tag to Shoes. Shoes finally tags in and quickly hits a boot to the face and his patented bulldog to the knee on Bull.

Light enters the fray as all four men fight in the ring I.O.D. are able to dominate once more and hit Shoes with their spike Pedigree, but decide that wasn't enough punishment and hit Light with the same move and then simultaneously pinned both guys for the 1, 2 and 3.

Winners: Icons of Dominance (Scott Grimm & John Bull w/The Boss)

Dragon Aisu vs Jekkel

Gabriel Grey shows favouritism towards his Damned Nation co-member, "Current 3CW Champion, 5 Time 3CW Champion and 1PW Tag Team Champion." Jekkel's introduction is pretty abrupt.

Match starts with both men chopping the hell out of each other. Aisu misses a lariat, unfortunately for him Jekkel doesn't. Aisu comes back with a kick to the leg and then grapevine's Jekkel's leg as the fans rally behind Jekkel. Uranagi by Aisu only manages a two count, Grey interjects himself in the match (distracting the Referee) which allows Aisu the opportunity to attack Jekkel from behind with a chop block.

Spinning toe hold by Aisu is quickly turned into a figure four as he looks for the submission victory, Jekkel is able to edge close (but not close enough) to the ropes before Aisu drags him back to mid-ring once again.

Jekkel seeing his predicament decides to reverse the pressure by rolling to his side (Aisu quickly grabs the ropes to escape the hold). Jekkel and Aisu exchange vicious kicks to the back, the fans chant "One-more-time" attempting a third Aisu lies down so Jekkel hits a senton splash. Jekkel hits a German suplex and huge powerbomb for a very close nearfall. Aisu is able to rally though and hits his face forward

DDT but on this occasion that only manages a near fall.

A Michinoku driver stops Aisu in his tracks, Jekkel then hits a double stomp off the top rope but amazingly that garners a two count only. Aisu distracts the Ref allowing Grey to hit Jekkel with his Cane, Aisu follows up with a Dragon suplex for the 1, 2 and 3.

Winner: Dragon Aisu

Fans boo loudly! Jekkel is able to gain a measure of revenge with a tombstone piledriver on Grey. Grey then makes the match Damned Nation vs Jekxodus for 7th October, fans voice their approval with chants of, "Jek-xodus."

Grey explains that Hugh Mungus isn't here because of car trouble but he still has an opponent for Exodus.

Enter 'Mr Bad Attitude' Martin Kirby.

Exodus vs 'Mr Bad Attitude' Martin Kirby

Fans chant "Martin Furby!" at Kirby, Kirby kicks Exodus and slams him to the mat. Aisu distracts the Referee which allows Kirby to hit Exodus with a chop block and kicks to the leg. Kirby continues the attack with a spinebuster which has seemingly setup the people's elbow. Instead of dropping an elbow he proceeds to slap Exodus across the face, that was a bad move!

Exodus hits Kirby with a vicious lariat and then a boot to the face, a chokeslam shortly follows and then Exodus puts Kirby down with the F6 for the 1, 2 and 3. Fans clap loudly and chant "Jek-xodus" as the match ends.

Winner: Exodus

Intergender Tag Match

Jetta & 'King of Funk' Cameron Kraze vs El Ligero & Violet

Kraze takes the Referee's glasses, puts them on and asks, "How blind are you?" Ligero checks the Ref for illegal objects. "Huss" chants are directed at Kraze (who is wearing furry boots), the match starts with Jetta and Violet in the ring (not for long though) as Jetta ducks the lock-up and tags in Kraze, Violet tags in El Ligero. Kraze attacks Ligero with a knee to the stomach and a fist to the face but as he attempts to 'Huss' he misses an elbow (which allows Ligero back in the match). Kraze covers his head but is caught with a dropkick to the back of his head followed by a standing moonsault for a two count.

Kraze tags Jetta, Jetta attempts Ligero's clapping flying head scissors but Ligero just throws her off (Jetta lands on her face, I believe that is when she bloodied her nose). Jetta distracts the Ref which allows for the double team, the fans rally behind Violet, Jetta suplexes Violet and stands on her hands. Jetta and Kraze double team once more (Jetta whips Violet into Kraze's elbow), this works on two separate occasions but on the third Jetta hits Kraze's elbow and with that the momentum has shifted to Violet and Ligero.

Violet drop toe hold's Jetta and hits a short arm clothesline before tagging Ligero (somehow the Ref missed it!), double clothesline has both women down.

Violet finally makes the tag to Ligero, Jetta tags in Kraze, Ligero turns a wheelbarrow into a stunner and hits a running boot for the 1, 2 – Jetta breaks up the fall.

Fans chant, "El-Ligero!" Ligero manages to fight back whipping Kraze into Violet who hits a jumping tornado DDT, Ligero follows this up with a top rope splash for the 1, 2 and 3.

Winners: El Ligero & Violet

Four Man Elimination Match

'100% Focused' Stiro vs 'Self-Professed Iron Man' Chris Stone vs 'Team Cream Leader' Ashton vs NWA UK Junior Heavyweight Champion Zack Sabre Jr (c)

Stiro enters the ring to loud boos. "I've come to Coventry to pay £1 for parking and wrestle three guys I have already beaten!" Chris Stone enters the ring next (Stiro and Stone shake hands), Ashton makes his way to the ring with chants of, "Ashton!" ringing in his ears, Zack Sabre Jr is the last to make his entrance, the fans greet him with "Zack!" chants. Sabre and Ashton shake hands.

Sabre and Stone start the match, Sabre is able to out muscle Stone and hits some vicious kicks before tagging in Ashton, Stone tags in Stiro. Ashton attempts a leg lock, Stiro rolls through into an armbar, Stiro synchs in the waistlock Ashton reverses this into a drop toe hold. Stiro locks in a headlock and then an armbar but once again Ashton rolls through, this time Stiro is wise to a possible reversal and drops his knee on Ashton's arm. Stiro puts Ashton in a chinlock but Ashton manages to reverse that too (into a pin for a close nearfall).

Stone pulls the rope and is admonished by the Ref, Ashton slaps Stone (Ref counts that as a tag). Fans chant "You both suck!" at Stone and Stiro. Stiro and Stone tag straight back out, Ashton and Sabre square off, Sabre locks in a Chicken wing on Ashton (but Ashton is able to reach the ropes). Ashton and Sabre exchange punches and kicks, Ashton whips Sabre into the ropes and hits a dropkick on Sabre for a two count. Sabre tags in Stone (Stiro taunts Ashton), Stone chokes Ashton with his boot and then leg drops Ashton's arm. Stone climbs to the top rope and hits a double stomp directly on to Ashton's arm and tags in Stiro.

Stiro and Stone isolate Ashton with consecutive tags, fans chant "Ashton" Ashton hits a bulldog and leg drop combination and tags in Sabre. Sabre runs through both men with vicious forearms, Ashton re-enters the ring but is quickly dumped out (with a back body drop on the wooden stage). Suicide dive by Sabre almost takes out the unsuspecting front row at ringside, all four men are back in the ring Ashton goes up top but Stone quickly follows and with a top rope Japanese armdrag Ashton's participation in the match is over, Stone covers him for the 1, 2 and 3.

Ashton has been eliminated at 16 minutes 31 seconds into the match.

Stiro and Stone double team Sabre. Stiro hits a Gory Guerrero special onto Stone's knee but as Stone attempts the pin Stiro stops him, Stiro attempts the pin (Stone stops him) and both men argue. Sabre kicks Stiro and quickly locks on the cross armbar which makes Stiro tap almost instantly.

Stiro has been eliminated at 18 minutes 41 seconds into the match.

"Zack" chants start up once more, Sabre responds with a roaring forearm that almost knocks Stone's head off, tiger suplex into a schoolboy roll up only manages a two count. Japanese armdrag by Stone (Sabre reaches the ropes), both men roll into a pin somehow Stone manages to lift his shoulder off the canvas before the 3 count and wins the match. Fans show their appreciation to Sabre (with loud clapping) as he leaves.

Winner: Chris Stone

Omar Ibrahim vs Edgar Stryfe

Omar takes the microphone. "I have travelled all the way from Turkish Cyprus to wrestle for you!" Stryfe enters to "E-Train" chants. "E-Train/O-Mar" duelling chants from the Triple X crowd. Stryfe takes Omar down with a waistlock he quickly changes into a headlock. Stryfe boots Omar in the stomach and then stands on him before hitting a big splash. Stryfe continues the attack with an inverted DDT leg drop combination. Omar comes back with a face wash variation (instead of using his boot, he uses his hand).

Omar reverses Stryfe's attempt at a diamond cutter into a spear but Stryfe lands too close to the ropes. Omar attempts a spear once again (although he hit it to perfection Stryfe amazingly brushes it off) and hits a diamond cutter/stunner for the 1, 2 and 3! The fans have a very mixed view on the ending with both boos and cheers directed towards Stryfe.

Winner: Edgar Stryfe

No DQ

'Bad Boy Of British wrestling' Jon Ryan vs 'Suicidal, Suicidal, Suicidal' Jimmy Havoc

"Jimmy!" chants greet Jimmy Havoc as he makes his way to the ring, fans also get behind Ryan (clapping loudly as he enters the ring). Both men exchange forearms to start the match, Havoc hits a dropkick (Ryan just brushes him off) a spinning wheel kick has more success. Ryan shows his strength by Gorilla press slamming Havoc from inside the ring to the wooden floor below! A Chair comes into play and is quickly smacked against Ryan's head but that only manages a two count. Havoc looks under the ring and pulls out a crutch and a frying pan, Ryan takes the crutch and smacks Havoc with it and then uses it to choke him.

Ryan manages to break the crutch over Havoc's back with a third shot! Havoc is able to rally though and quickly uses the frying pan to good effect (with two vicious shots to Ryan's head). Havoc ascends the turnbuckle for a splash but is met by a chair to the face. "Jimmy/Ryan" duelling chants from the Triple X faithful, Havoc sets up the chair while Ryan is crotched on the top rope (Havoc uses the chair to springboard and hits Ryan with a kick knocking him to the outside). Havoc follows that with a high cross body, Ryan recovers and both men proceed to brawl around Jumping Jaks.

Havoc is able to reverse Ryan's momentum with a backdrop on the wooden floor! Ryan frustrated throws Havoc down the stairs to the wooden floor below. Ryan then picks up a wooden board (from under the ring), Ryan then places the board between a chair and the turnbuckle, with Havoc down Ryan climbs the turnbuckle. Havoc crotches Ryan and then hits a double stomp through the board and chair on Ryan but only manages a two count. Havoc pulls out another wooden board and sets it up in the opposite corner this time Ryan is able to hit Havoc with a T-Bone suplex through the wooden board 1, 2 but Havoc is able to get his shoulder up.

Ryan returns under the ring once more (he picks up three steel chairs and a metal case) Ryan hits Havoc's head with the metal case three times!! He then sets up the chairs, Ryan picks Havoc up and stands on the chairs and hits a Ryan-oku driver for the 1, 2 and 3!

Winner: 'Bad Boy Of British Wrestling' Jon Ryan

Fans clap loudly for Ryan, Ryan shows Havoc respect by shaking his hand, which elicits a loud cheer for Havoc also followed by "Jimmy" chants from the fans. "Triple X" chants follow and as Grey returns to the ring the fans chant "Omar's better" (Omar has been a ring announcer at previous Triple X shows).

The match I paid to see (Four Man Elimination) was worth the price of admission alone, it was a tremendous match between four of the best up and comers in the U.K. Zack Sabre Jr vs Chris Stone is a match I may just pay another £7 to see!

Ryan vs Havoc was the other stand out match as the two absolutely brutalized each other for the fans entertainment. Lots of entertainment and two top notch matches made Triple X 'Jak'ed Up' a very good show.

Leicester Pro Wrestling

Date: Friday 21st September 2007
Time: 8:00pm
Attendance: 50
Price: Adults £5, Kids £3
Location: Minworth Social Club, Robinson's Way, Sutton Coldfield.

AJ Kid Irish is your host for this evening.

John Bull vs Gangsta

The Firm enters (Jay Icon/LGT/The Bouncer/The Boss), The Boss takes the microphone "As a result of not beating Jay Icon here is the newest member of the firm corporate John Bull." AJ "With 5 of you, you could be a Spice Girls tribute band" then quickly exits the ring. Gangsta makes his way to the ring, the fans cheer.

The bell rings Bull attempts to tie-up but Gangsta is too quick, he evades the tie-up on two separate occasions. Bull finally gets a hold of Gangsta but not for long as Gangsta forces him back into the corner and quickly hits Bull with a superkick to the back of the head, sending Bull to the outside. Bull re-enters the ring, Gangsta hits a kick to the stomach and a swinging DDT which sends Bull to the outside once more. As Gangsta attempts to capitalize The Bouncer trips him up.

Bull seeing the momentum has shifted quickly hits a big powerslam, and a big splash for a two count. LGT distracts the Referee (this allows Bull to choke Gangsta), when Bull is done choking The Bouncer takes over. Bull locks Gangsta in the camel clutch, the fans rally behind Gangsta. As Gangsta looks to be fading he finds some energy and fights back with a barrage of punches and a knee to the head. With Bull in the corner Gangsta hits with a step up kick, Bull quickly returns though with a vicious clothesline! Bull follows up with a suplex and a big splash but only manages a two count.

First rope splash by Bull 1, 2, Gangsta is able to get his shoulder up, Bull attempts a second rope splash and misses. Fans rally behind Gangsta once more as the Ref counts both men out, he manages to get to 7 before Gangsta nips up. Gangsta hits Bull with a clothesline, shoulder block and a step up kick in quick succession. Bull hits Gangsta with a spear for the 1, 2 and 3.

Winner: Corporate John Bull w/The Firm

Match Time: 7 minutes

This was a good big man vs little man match, Gangsta against all odds (mainly The Firm's interference) almost pulled out the win but Bull's strength advantage told in the end as he was able to gain the victory.

The Metal Militia (Axel Adams & Pure Xtasy) vs Tucker & Poison

Militia attack Tucker and Poison from behind, Tucker takes a spill to the outside. Xtasy locks Poison in a full nelson, Axel attempts to punch Poison, Poison moves out of the way and Adams almost hits his tag partner. Poison stamps on Adams's toes and tags in Tucker. Tucker hits an Armdrag, Japanese armdrag, kick to the back and a dropkick to Adams's face in quick succession. Tucker tags in Poison who goes to work on Adams's arm with a wristlock, twisting it in different directions before tagging Tucker in once more.

Tucker takes Adams to the mat and hits a knee drop to the arm, he then takes the arm and hits a variation of the dragon screw, as Tucker is setting up another attack Xtasy grabs him and drops him neck first on the top rope. Adams tags in Xtasy and they quickly hit a double clothesline on Tucker, Adams chokes Tucker and then distracts the Referee (by taunting Poison) allowing Xtasy to do the same. Adams pins Tucker but only manages a two count (Militia complain about a slow count). Adams tags in Xtasy, they continue to isolate Poison whilst trading tags back and forth.

Nonchalant cover by Adams gains a two count, Poison tags in Tucker. Fans chant "Tucker," Tucker hits a double cross body block on the Militia, Tucker tags in Poison whilst Xtasy tags in Adams. Poison hits a double noggin knocker on the Militia, Tucker out of nowhere hits Poison with an enzuguri and leaves ringside! Seemingly come back to his senses he returns only to get downed with Poison's TKO

(Poison leaves ringside), the Militia take advantage of the situation quickly hitting the D.O.A. for the 1, 2 and 3.

Winners: The Metal Militia (Axel Adams & Pure Xtasy)

Match Time: 11 minutes

First time seeing Tucker, I was impressed. Pretty solid tag match, Tucker turning on Poison came out of nowhere, I hadn't noticed any bad feeling between the two.

British Iron Man Championship Match

No DQ

L.G.T. w/The Firm vs Jekkel (c)

LGT enters with The Firm but decides to go it alone (sending The Firm to the back) LGT stretches as Jekkel waits in the ring. Jekkel charges at LGT, LGT quickly exits the ring. LGT returns, walking straight up to Jekkel before spitting in his face, and then runs away. Jekkel catches up with him and hits with a couple of shoulder blocks and a powerslam, LGT retreats once again (this time Jekkel follows). LGT attempts an Irish whip but Jekkel reverses sending LGT head first into the steel ringpost. Jekkel asks if anyone has a shoe! A fan gladly obliges (Jekkel hits LGT with said shoe to the head).

The two wrestlers continue brawling until they leave the room, moments later they are back. LGT rams Jekkel's head in an ice bucket. Both men return to the ring, LGT hits a chop block on Jekkel (as he is entering the ring). LGT then focuses his entire offence on Jekkel's legs grounding the big man. LGT chokes Jekkel with his boot and hands and then leaves the ring in search of a weapon. He comes back with a steel chair, LGT throws the chair at Jekkel (Jekkel catches it and throws it directly into LGT's face).

LGT hides behind the Referee, so much for non-interference (The Boss & Corporate John Bull make their way to ringside), LGT takes the chair and aims for Jekkel but hits Bull in the head, Jekkel quickly follows up with the Jekkel driver for the 1, 2 and 3.

Match Time: 6 minutes

Winner and STILL British Iron Man Champion: Jekkel (c)

Decent match, Jekkel's power vs LGT's brains and The Firm's interference. LGT almost had it won but Jekkel's power allowed him to pull out the win and retain his British Iron Man Championship.

Jay Icon w/The Firm vs Ronin w/Mini Ronin

"I'm Jay Icon!" shouts Icon. Mini Ronin takes the microphone; "Ronin is so fast that when he turns off a light he is in bed before it goes dark."

Icon attacks Ronin from the start (to little effect) sensing this Icon backs away, Ronin follows and hits Icon with clubs to the neck and back. Ronin Irish whips Icon and follows up with a big splash in the corner. Icon's down but Ronin isn't finished, big elbow and powerslam on Icon, Ronin locks in an armbar but The Firm help Icon to the ropes. Ronin slaps on a full nelson changing into a half-nelson/chinlock, Icon rams Ronin back into the corner following up with elbows to the face and attempted punch which Ronin catches and locks in the chinlock once more.

Ronin hits his patented swinging Rock Bottom 1, 2 no! The Firm interfere again! They ram Ronin groin first into the steelpost, Icon repeatedly stamps on Ronin's legs and then distracts the Referee allowing The Firm to continue their attack, Icon pins Ronin 1, 2! "Ronin" chants from the fans, Icon continues his assault to the legs of Ronin, Figure four leg lock by Icon, Bouncer pulls on Icon's arms to give leverage. Ronin is able to use his strength to reverse the pressure onto Icon (Icon is able to get to the ropes).

Ronin fires back with two chops to the throat, repeated stomps and a kick to the back of Icon's legs. The Boss distracts the Ref allowing LGT to hit a low blow, Mini Ronin hits Icon with the Singapore cane, Ronin hits the big splash 1, 2 and 3.

Match Time: 10 minutes

Winner: Ronin w/Mini Ronin

Good big man vs little man match, Ronin's weight advantage was the difference in this match despite Icon's sound offence to Ronin's legs and interference from The Firm.

Handicap Match

Mad Mike vs Carnage & Aphrodite

"Mad Mike!" chants from the crowd. Mike and Aphrodite start the match, Mike attempts to tie-up but Aphrodite ducks out. Mike has Aphrodite in a waistlock then changes into a headlock Aphrodite grabs the ropes and tags in Carnage. Kick to the stomach, back chop and choke on the ropes allows Carnage to change the momentum of the match. Mike fights back, with Carnage down in the corner Mike hits his patented dropkick to the groin, Carnage struggles back towards his corner to make a tag to Aphrodite. Mike stops Carnage in his tracks with an atomic drop and a Manhattan drop in quick succession.

Carnage relieves the pressure with a club to Mike's neck followed by a pump handle slam allowing him to make the tag to Aphrodite. Aphrodite hits an elbow drop and tags back out to Carnage. Carnage nonchalantly covers Mike (Mike's foot is on the ropes) so the Ref breaks up the count. Carnage tags back out to Aphrodite, Mike attempts a kick - Aphrodite catches it and reverses into a leg lock. Mike makes it back to his feet and while looking at Carnage delivers a huge powerslam on Aphrodite, a Russian leg sweep follows but as the pinfall is being made Carnage pushes Mike off.

"Mike" chants from the crowd, Aphrodite makes the tag. Mike gets a second wind hitting a running clothesline on Carnage and a belly to back suplex on Aphrodite, before nailing a back body drop on Carnage's & Aphrodite's second at ringside. Mike springboards of a ringside chair to hit Carnage with a dropkick to the face. Carnage returns to the ring and quickly tags in Aphrodite, Aphrodite slaps Mike across the face and lands a running leg drop for a two count, Mike reverses into a two count of his own.

Aphrodite makes the tag, Mike runs at Carnage and with a clothesline sends himself and Carnage over the top rope to the floor. Mike climbs from a chair to a wooden ledge, running and connecting with a double axe handle to Carnage, he attempts to do the same once more. This time Carnage catches Mike and rams him back first into the steel ringpost. Carnage rolls Mike into the ring and tags in Aphrodite, she poses for the crowd, Mike regains some composure and attempts a powerslam, Carnage grabs Mike's legs allowing Aphrodite to fall on top of Mike and gain the 1, 2 and 3!

Match Time: 13 minutes

Winners: Aphrodite & Carnage

Aftermath:
Carnage isn't done though and lands with a second rope slingshot body splash to the fallen Mike, Carnage and Aphrodite make their way to the back. Mike follows and brings Carnage back to the ring quickly locking on a crossface to Carnage which makes him immediately tap out. Mike takes the microphone. "Me and you, Carnage, Last Man Standing at Shard End!" Carnage accepts.

Good match between two of the premier LPW wrestlers, Aphrodite looked decent in the limited

time she spent in the ring. Mike being pinned by
Aphrodite was a huge shock!

Dante Corinthian Vandal vs Silverado

Vandal while posing for the crowd hits his head on
the ceiling, Silverado enters to "Silver-ado" chants
from the LPW fans.

Both men lock-up in the centre of the ring Vandal
drops down and trips Silverado, Armdrag and a
dropkick in quick succession by Silverado in return.
Silverado poses for the crowd, Vandal attempts a
sneak attack from behind but gets hit with an elbow,
after a delayed reaction he falls to the canvas (this
elicits laughter from the crowd). Vandal returns with
a European uppercut and a big boot sending
Silverado to the outside. Vandal Irish whips
Silverado, Silverado reverses and Vandal runs
shoulder first into the steel ringpost.

Back in the ring Vandal downs Silverado with a
series of power moves (powerslam, backbreaker and
sideslam in seamless fashion). Fans clap for
Silverado, Silverado responds with a head scissors to
Vandal, attempting a spear but Vandal is unmoved.
Vandal points to the crowd, Silverado slaps him on
the back of the head. Silverado attempts a sunset flip
but instead of the pin Silverado pulls Vandal's
trousers down!

Fans laugh hysterically but Vandal's anger allows
him to turn the match, clubs to the neck and back
(Vandal pulls his trousers back up) are quickly
followed up by a release German suplex. Vandal
measures Silverado and hits a number of short arm
clotheslines with the last one flipping Silverado! 1, 2,

but Vandal pulls Silverado up off the canvas. "Silverado!" chants once more, Vandal locks Silverado in the cobra clutch submission and repeatedly drops Silverado's head onto his knee, with the cobra clutch still locked in the Ref checks the arm, it drops three times and the match is over!

Match Time: 7 minutes

Winner: Dante Corinthian Vandal

Aftermath:
Vandal whips Silverado into the turnbuckle upside down, and poses for the crowd. Once again hilariously he bangs his head on the ceiling! Vandal picks Silverado up and hits a big boot. Fans clap for Silverado.

Pretty good back and forth match for a short while, Dante's embarrassment was the turning point of the match, his anger fuelled him towards victory.

LPW Championship Match

'Jamaica's #1 Bobsledder' Derice Coffie vs The Bouncer w/The Firm (c)

AJ Kid Irish asks a fan at ringside, "What's better, English or Irish?" to which the fan responds, "English!" which causes the fans to laugh.

LGT and Jay Icon enter the ring, they want to do the introductions of The Bouncer. "Entering is the Phoenix City Champion and LPW Champion - The Bouncer, accompanied by the greatest manager ever The Boss!"

"Coming from the 1988 Olympics, Jamaica's #1 Bobsledder" Derice Coffie."

Both men lock-up, Bouncer gets the advantage and dumps Coffie to the outside although The Firm is on that side of the ring they strangely decline to interfere in the match, Coffie decides to attack them all and returns to the ring. Coffie hits with a shoulder block but bounces directly off The Bouncer. Coffie follows up with a dropkick and an armdrag with better success. "Make some noise" Coffie asks the crowd, they gladly oblige. Coffie runs towards the ropes, LGT trips him and LGT and Icon attack Coffie as Bull distracts the Referee.

Bouncer responds with a punch to Coffie's head and a backbreaker for a two count. Bouncer follows up with a kick to each of the different pressure points on Coffie's body. "Coffie" chants from the crowd, Bouncer quickly hits a knee to the head and with his knee exposed another knee to Coffie's head. Bouncer Irish whips Coffie into the ropes and locks in the sleeper hold, Coffie looks like he is fading, but suddenly springs to life with a wheelbarrow into a bulldog "Baldy" chants from the LPW fans directed at The Bouncer (Bouncer puts on a cap!).

Coffie attempts a high cross body but Bouncer catches him and dumps him to the outside (on top of The Firm), The Firm ram Coffie back first into the ringpost and throw Coffie back in the ring. Bouncer hits with a neckbreaker as The Firm taunt the crowd.

Leg snap by Bouncer, Coffie struggles to his feet and is met with a fireman's carry onto Bouncer's knees for a two count. Coffie is back on his feet once more and with a series of quick punches downs the Bouncer, Coffie ascends the turnbuckle and in the process knocks a light bulb and the lights in Minworth Social club go completely out!

The Firm sense the opportunity to once again interfere, this time Coffie is wise to the situation and trips each member as they enter. With all of The Firm in position Coffie sits down and directs a bobsled run! Although difficult to see, the fans who did, laugh hysterically once more. The lights come back on, the LPW Championship is in the ring, Coffie annoyed at the constant interference looks like he is going to take matters into his own hands (as he picks up the Title belt).

The Firm distract the Referee once more, Coffie and Bouncer throw the title at each other and feign injury and when the Ref turns around threw the title at him! With the Referee distracted again Bouncer hits Coffie with the Phoenix City Championship, 1, 2 and 3! Fans clap for Coffie as he leaves.

Match Time: 11 minutes

Winner and STILL LPW Champion: The Bouncer w/The Firm (c)

This match had it all from interference, good wrestling, a bobsled run in a wrestling ring is something I never thought I would see! The lights going out and back on again added to the drama, trading the title back and forth while feigning injury elicited a lot of laughter from the crowd.

Pretty solid show from top to bottom, there wasn't anything that you would say wow that was great, but the wrestling was of a good standard, the comedy was tremendous and all in all it was a fun show.

Legends Wrestling League
(LWL Aftershock Report Part One)

Date: Tuesday 25th September 2007
Time: 7:30pm
Attendance: 39
Price: Adults £5, £4 with LWL Flyer (Downloadable from http://www.lwluk.co.uk) Kids £3
Location: Legends Members Club, Oxley Street, Wolverhampton, West Midlands.

Motor Mouth Mike is your host for this evening.

Mike introduces Matthew J. Stark, the new commissioner of LWL to crown the LWL Champion. "I'm not happy about this, but it has to be done."
    Loud cheering as Mat Mensa makes his way to the ring. "I'll hand over this LWL Championship if you give me that National Pride Championship," states Stark.
    "Should I?" Mensa asks the fans, they reply with a loud "Yes!" so Mensa hands over the National Pride Championship and is handed back the LWL Championship.
    Steve Valentino makes his way to the ring (the fans greet him with boos), he attempts to talk but the microphone cuts out! "I'm National Pride #1 Contender!" Valentino shouts. Valentino then attacks Mensa with the help of Danny Devine, Dan Ryder (Crowd cheers loudly) comes out to even up the odds. Fans cheer for Mensa as he leaves.

Stark continues, "Here are my new enforcers The Firm."

"Pee Wee Herman!" chants directed towards the Referee. The fans boo The Firm as they enter Stark closes by saying, "The Firm will be the most dominant men in LWL History!" Carnage and Kris Navarro make their way to the ring (Crowd cheers loudly).

The Firm (TGR & The Bouncer) w/The Boss vs Carnage & Kris Navarro

Carnage stands behind TGR as he turns around he almost jumps out of his boots! Bouncer enters, TGR distracts Carnage allowing Bouncer to attack from behind, Navarro attempts a save but gets double teamed for his troubles as Carnage is dumped to the outside. Double Russian legsweep by The Firm on Navarro, TGR stamps on Navarro (The fans rally behind Navarro). TGR tags in Bouncer who proceeds to kick Navarro and attack Carnage allowing a double team once more in the form of a Backbreaker/second Rope elbow combination.

Big slam and leg drop by Bouncer. "We want Carnage!" chant starts up. Bouncer tags in TGR, he quickly hits a running avalanche in the corner into a bulldog for a two count. Frustrated he pins Navarro again (one count), and again (another one count) and once more (one count). "One plus one plus one equals three!" he tells the Ref! TGR chokes Navarro with his boot, Carnage enters allowing The Firm to double team Navarro again, with a wishbone leg splitter unfortunately at this point the ring breaks!

Carnage attacks the Bouncer, and he, Navarro and The Firm brawl around the hall. Carnage hits Bouncer with a powerslam on a solid wooden table. TGR hits his patented Stamp/Senton on Navarro on another table. Extraordinarily the match continues (in the broken ring), Carnage suplexes Bouncer on the ringside floor, The Firm combine once more for a double noggin knocker on Carnage and Navarro, TGR and Navarro return the ring and with a vicious Chokebomb (by TGR) the 1, 2 and 3 count is made and The Firm are your winners.

Fans boo loudly at The Firm and cheer for Carnage and Navarro as they leave.

Winners: The Firm (TGR & The Bouncer) w/The Boss

Match Time: 7 minutes

This had the makings of a good match, The Firm looked extremely dominant in the early going, with Carnage aching for the tag when the ring broke. This could have been turned into a good tag match unfortunately just as it seemed to get going the ring broke and then it was just a case of finishing the match, which they did.

Intermission as LWL staff attempted to fix the broken ring, unfortunately it was to no avail. The show was cancelled, the fans were refunded and the show was rescheduled for two weeks' time.

This was a one match show (In every sense of the word!), with the ring breaking in the first match. Despite the best efforts of the LWL staff the show had to be cancelled, and is now rescheduled for two weeks' time. It had the makings of a good show and I for one will be back in two weeks to see how it concludes.

Anti-Watershed Wrestling

Date: Thursday 27th September 2007
Time: 8:00pm
Attendance: 72
Price: £5
Location: Irish Centre, Digbeth, Birmingham, West Midlands

Stu Smith is your host for this evening, he announces that Referee Potter is making his wrestling debut (fans cheer wildly!)

Ashe Steele vs 'Scorpion' Bill Duffy

As Ashe makes his way to the ring the fans chant "Steele," Duffy is booed as he enters and doesn't help matters by spitting and pouring beer on the fans!

Motor Mouth Mike makes his way to the stage, and seems to be scouting talent. The bell rings to start the match, Steele poses for the crowd (Duffy attacks from behind) with a low blow and whips Steele into the corner, but misses with the attempted running elbow. Steele counters with hiptosses and a dropkick in quick succession.

Steele has Duffy in the corner and attempts the 10 punch but Steele pushes him off and knees him in stomach, following up with a dropkick to the face. Stomps follow as a section of the crowd chants "We want Axel" (Showing Metal Militia's Axel Adams support after he recently was let go by AWW), European uppercuts by Duffy, Duffy is distracted by the crowd. Dory Funk Jr. roll up by Steele out of the corner for a two count, fans rally behind Steele, a kick to Steele's stomach puts a halt to his comeback and Duffy follows up with a suplex for a two count.

Illegal choke by Duffy, snapmere follows with a vicious kick to the head. Clothesline attempt by Duffy Steele reverses into a flying head scissors.

"Not as good as Axel!" chant the AWW fans, both men are back to their feet, Steele blocks a Duffy punch and returns with an Enzuguri for a two count. Fans clap for Steele, Steele suplexes Duffy. "Give him a chop!" shout the fans. "Chop, yeah?" Steele replies, the fans shout in unison, "Yes!" so he does just that.

Steele climbs the ropes (Duffy pulls the Ref in front of him) and then pushes the Ref into the ropes crotching Steele on the top rope, Steele falls to the mat, Duffy follows up with a pin and his feet on the ropes allow the leverage to gain 1, 2 and 3 count.

Match Time: 7 minutes

Winner: 'Scorpion' Bill Duffy

AWW fans made their feelings heard with chants for The Metal Militia's Axel Adams, but that didn't take away from a pretty solid match between Steele and Duffy, a good back and forth contest between the two men that really could have gone either way. With the way the match finished a rematch should be on the cards and I for one welcome that.

The Young Gunns (Tommy Gunn/Geraden) vs Ronin & 'Jamaica's 1 Bobsledder' Derice Coffie (aka Ashton Smith)

"You sold out!" chants directed at Stu Smith as he returns to announce the next match.

He mentions the return of Tommy Gunn (the fans are incredibly happy with that!). Gunn/Geraden are cheered loudly as they enter (Geraden is wearing Ex-AWW Tucker's 'Smile' T-Shirt and once in the ring shows his support for The Metal Militia by posing like Axel Adams), Ronin and Derice Coffie get a similar reception from the fans. Derice makes the fans to do the Jamaican wave when he walks by each side of the ring, Ronin stops him from continuing it in the ring, so Coffie hilariously stands behind Ronin waving, and runs away when Ronin turns around.

Motor Mouth Mike once again makes his way to the stage. "Let's hear some noise!" shouts Coffie, fans reply by chanting, "Tommy!" loudly. Gunn squares up to Ronin! Ronin floors Gunn with shoulder blocks, Gunn attempts another and a dropkick but they have little effect on the Japanese Assassin. Gunn tags in Geraden. "Geraden!" chants by the AWW fans, Ronin tags in Coffie. Armdrag, Japanese armdrag, hiptoss and dropkick in lightning quick fashion by Geraden. Irish whip attempt by Geraden Coffie reverses into 'Feel the rhythm, feel the rhyme' and clothesline's Geraden before tagging Ronin in once more.

Ronin hits Geraden with an elbow to the face for a two count, elbows to the neck follow as the fans once more chant "Geraden," Ronin puts Geraden in a headlock and illegally punches him in the head.

Swinging Rock bottom into the turnbuckle on Geraden! Followed by a uranagi for a two count. Geraden fights back but as he is building momentum Ronin pulls him down to the mat by his hair. Ronin attacks Gunn and punches Geraden in the head dropping him to the mat once more. Ronin hits a huge powerslam "Tag in Ashton" chants by the AWW crowd, so Ronin does just that.

Knee to Geraden's face followed by a vicious superkick, fans are in awe! Wheelbarrow drop to Geraden, Gunn attempts save and gets hiptossed for his troubles. They are in position for the Bobsled Run! Unfortunately for the AWW fans Ronin stops it causing the fans to boo loudly. Geraden finally makes the tag to Gunn, Gunn takes Coffie out with a leg lariat and attempts to whip Ronin, Ronin reverses but Gunn slips out and hits a top rope double axe handle to the back of Ronin for a two count.

"Let's go Young Gunns," chant starts up, flying head scissors by Geraden on Coffie takes Coffie to the outside, Geraden quickly follows up with a flip dive over the top rope onto Coffie. Gunn/Geraden use this as a chance to double team Ronin, Coffie inadvertently pulls the top rope down sending Ronin sprawling over, Gunn runs and hits a picture perfect Fosbury flop onto Coffie and Ronin! Gunn pushes Ronin back in the ring, Geraden hits a scissors kick to the back of Ronin's head, Gunn ascends the turnbuckle and hits a twisting splash for the 1, 2 and 3! Tommy Gunn has pinned Ronin!!

Fans clap loudly for Geraden & Gunn as Ronin and Coffie disagree about who was to blame for the loss, Coffie leaves the ring. Fans show respect to Ronin with applause also.

Match Time: 9 minutes

Winners: The Young Gunns (Geraden & Tommy Gunn)

Bold prediction time, the Young Gunns (Tommy Gunn & Geraden) are going to be money for AWW! They put forth a tremendous tag team display in this match, I believed before the match they would make a good tag team but they even exceeded my expectations.

Derice Coffie's debut was pretty solid and the fans seem to warm to him right from the start. I didn't in a million years believe that Tommy Gunn would pin Ronin, but I guess that's why they say anything can happen in Pro Wrestling!

'The Metrosexual' Danny Devine vs British Born Steele

Devine sprays the fans with deodorant and a female in the crowd throws a pair of her underwear at him, fans approach asking for a spray, Devine gladly obliges. BBS enters to loud cheers, slapping the fans hands as he makes his way around the ring.

The two combatants lock-up, BBS gets the advantage and backs Devine into the corner, when the Ref asks for a clean break he obliges. Devine takes the advantage in the second lock-up but when asked to break he slaps BBS, as BBS attempts retribution Devine cowardly backs off. Devine misses with a chop, chop by BBS, knees to the chest followed by an armdrag and a wristlock in seamless fashion.

Devine is able to reverse out but the attempted spear misses and BBS locks on an armbar and transitions into a wristlock once more, twisting the wrist and then leg dropping it. Devine escapes the ring with the wristlock amazingly still locked in as both men leave the ring! BBS chops Devine as he is still attempting to release himself from BBS's wristlock.

"One more?" BBS asks the crowd. The fans reply, "Yes!" so he obliges. BBS then rams Devine's arm into the steel ringpost to resounding "B-B-S!" chants, Devine finally turns the tables by wrapping BBS's leg around the ringpost to a violent thump!

Devine wraps BBS's leg around the post once more. Devine and BBS return to the ring, Devine puts BBS in the corner and wraps BBS's injured leg in the ropes, trapping the ankle and knee. Leg breaker by Devine, kicks to the leg and the Stryker-lock submission on BBS. BBS refuses to tap and although struggling manages to reach the ropes, Devine refuses to break the hold. "Pull me off, Ref!" he shouts. BBS uses this opportunity to surprise Devine with an enziguri kick, quick punches, a flying clothesline and a leg lariat in quick succession.

"Militia" chants from the crowd, Devine cuts BBS off with a boot to the stomach, into a northern lights suplex and into a pinfall with the Perfectplex but BBS kicks out!

"We want Axel!" chants followed by, "B-B-S!" chants and lastly, "Xtasy!" chants from the AWW fans. Spike DDT by BBS but Devine manages to get his shoulder up, BBS reverses a Devine punch, kick to Devine's knee and a Perfectplex of his own for a two count. Fans feel Ref has slow counted and let him know with chants of, "Slow count."

Devine mockingly asks the fans, "Is this all he's got?" BBS fires back with ill-advised kicks to Devine with his bad leg!

He realizes the error of his ways and corrects them with a kick to Devine with his good leg for a two count. "Yeah!" BBS shouts as he attempts a tornado DDT, Devine reverses it into a spine buster.

Devine locks BBS in the single leg crab. "Daily Metro!" chants from the crowd, BBS once again struggles but manages to find his way to the ropes to break the hold. BBS pulls himself up by the turnbuckles, Devine charges and misses BBS quickly hits the Backcracker! Both men are down Ref starts the 10 count, he makes it to 5 (fans rally behind BBS) Devine hits a vicious knee breaker directly to the mat and locks in the single leg crab once more.

"B-B-S!" chants from the fans Devine uses the Referee's impaired vision (Ref is checking BBS's arm) to cheat by putting both his hand and foot on the rope. "Potter won't have seen it!" chants by the AWW faithful. BBS manages to somehow get to the ropes once more, Devine attempts an avalanche, misses and is almost pinned with the schoolboy pin (two count).

Devine knocks BBS down once more and locks in the Sharpshooter and with his hands on the ropes once again (It looked like the Referee saw it and didn't break the hold!) BBS has no choice but to tap out!

Devine leaves with the underwear the woman threw at him, fans clap BBS's valiant performance as he returns to his feet and exits the ring and "B-B-S!" chants ring in his ears as he makes his way backstage.

Match Time: 12 minutes

Winner: 'The Metrosexual' Danny Devine

I loved every single second of that – that was an incredible match! BBS's resilience and fortitude was a sight to behold, as he valiantly fought through the pain to try and win the match.

Devine's offence was incredibly sound, attacking the legs and working them down to breaking point, although the win was tainted, it is still a win.

The finish of the match looks like it is pointing towards a rematch and I for one can't wait until Devine v BBS 2!

INTERMISSION

Mad Dog Maxx, Nick Knight & Latz w/Aphrodite vs Lee Hunter, Marcus Kool & Dan Ryder

Maxx, Latz and Knight enter to resounding boos from the AWW crowd. Maxx runs around the ring like a crazed lunatic. Hunter and Kool make their entrances, it's clear who the fans want to see with "Ryder" chants even before Dan Ryder makes his entrance! Ryder, Kool and Hunter rush the ring, and chaos ensues.

Ryder gets dumped to the outside by Maxx, Knight knocks Kool to outside also. Knight throws Aphrodite's whip away! She goes to get it. Kool and Knight square off in a chop fest, the 6 man brawl goes into the crowd and onto some unlucky fans laps. Kool takes a powerslam directly to the wooden floor, at this point Maxx is chopping Ryder, Knight takes over and whips Ryder straight into the steel ringpost. Maxx chops Hunter in the throat, Knight clotheslines Ryder, Kool tries to punch Maxx but he manages to cover up.

This action is crazy and very difficult to follow! Finally Latz and Hunter decide to take the action back to the ring, meanwhile Kool low blows Knight and hits him on the back of the head with a steel chair. Flying forearms by Hunter and a spinning heel kick knock Latz down "Hunter" chants from the crowd. Maxx attacks from behind with a kick to Hunter's head, Kool tries to enter the ring in defence of Hunter but only allows for a two on one attack by Maxx's team, Maxx slaps his hand (behind referee's back, like a tag). Fans chant "Latz, Latz!"

Dropkick to Hunter's face by Maxx, who then tags out to Knight, fans chant "Marcus" hoping Kool would be tagged in. Knight chokes Hunter in the corner. "Let's go, Hunter!" chants from a section of the AWW crowd, another section chants, "Let's go Mad Dog!"

Knight sets up Hunter in a tree of woe, Latz delivers a dropkick to Hunter's face, Maxx kicks Hunter in the back but Hunter manages to kick out of the resulting pinfall attempt at two. Latz distracts Kool and Team Mad Dog triple team Hunter behind the Referee's back.

"Hunter" chants once again, Kool spits at Latz, Latz tags in Maxx. Maxx gets telegraphed going for a back body drop by Hunter with a boot to the face, Maxx quickly quashes Hunter's momentum with a

Polish hammer and tags back out to Latz. Kool distracts the Ref once again trying to help but in the end hindering his partner. Triple team attack again by Team Maxx, Knight knocks Ryder off the apron, Maxx taunts Ryder allowing for yet another three on one beat down of Lee Hunter!

Snapmere and a fist to the face off of the second rope by Maxx. "Let's go, Hunter!" chants from the fans. Chops by Maxx, Hunter manages to hit a desperation Enzuguri Hunter lunges towards Kool and Ryder and tags both men, Maxx does the same to Knight and Latz. Double back drop on Maxx, then Ryder hits a dropkick on Latz and follows up with a standing moonsault, Kool hits a senton on Latz and then Hunter returns and while Latz is being double suplexed by Ryder and Kool hits a high cross body on Latz! "That was awesome!" chant from the crowd.

Ryder squares off against Knight, Knight lays Ryder out with a spinebuster, Kool knocks Knight down with a superkick, Latz hits his finishing move the Unprettier on Kool. Hunter then quickly hits a facebuster on Latz, Maxx takes Hunter out with a lariat, dropkick by Ryder sends Maxx to the ringside floor. Ryder ascends the turnbuckle and hits a picture perfect 450 from the ring onto the wrestlers below! Crowd is awe struck by that… Kool and Maxx make it back to the ring, Maxx falls into the ropes (between the middle and top) Kool hits the 0121 on Maxx (Birmingham's area code).

Following up with a second rope moonsault but that manages to get a close two count but nothing more. "Let's go, Marcus!" chants from the crowd, Kool jumps off the ropes but Maxx is waiting with a Manhattan drop, and quickly follows up with a pulling piledriver for the 1, 2 and 3! Fans clap Dan Ryder's team, Knight and Latz pose as Ryder and Hunter check on the fallen Marcus Kool, fans applaud for Ryder's team once more as they leave.

Match Time: 15 minutes

Winners: Mad Dog Maxx, Nick Knight & Latz w/Aphrodite

That was chaotic! Incredible atmosphere in the Irish Centre that actually sent chills down my spine.

Although the match was to further the feud between Mad Dog Maxx and Dan Ryder, the other competitors performed well with Hunter exceeding my expectations with his resilience.

The match had pretty much everything. Brawling, high flying (especially the 450 from Ryder to the outside), that was a wow moment, a very good six man tag that just worked.

'Wonderkid' Jonny Storm vs 'Human Hate Machine' Moralez

Stu Smith announces, "Still to come we have Potter wrestling!" The fans erupt! "Potter, Potter!" they chant.

The fans boo Moralez on his entrance so he uses this as an opportunity to berate the fans of AWW. Jonny Storm gets a better reception as the fans cheer loudly on his entrance and clap along to his theme tune, the Referee checks Moralez for foreign objects as the fans chant, "Never seen a salad!"

Lock-up Moralez pushes Storm into the corner and slaps Storm, second lock-up this time Storm reverses and pushes Moralez into the corner but Moralez just pushes Storm off.

Moralez lifts Storm for a powerbomb but Storm fights out and nails the hurricanrana on Moralez, Storm follows up with a flying head scissors which dumps Moralez to the outside of the ring. Moralez rolls straight back in the ring and charges at Storm, Storm lowers the top rope sending Moralez to the outside again. Moralez re-enters the ring and cobblers Storm, Storm arm drags Moralez and transitions into a wristlock, Moralez reverses out into an armbar of his own on Storm. "Jonny" chant starts up, Storm moves up into a headstand and reverses out of it!

Storm attempts a rope flip but Moralez cuts him off by crotching him on the top rope, Storm gets his arm of the canvas at the count of two. Moralez shoulder blocks Storm's lower back in the corner and when the Referee tries to break it up, Moralez berates the Official. "Jonny" chants once again, Moralez chokes Storm with his boot and rubs his elbow in Storm's face before breaking on the fourth count (of five) by the Ref, Storm battles back with chops but once again Moralez cuts Storm off with a forearm to the face.

"Who's the greatest Wrestler you have seen tonight?" asks Moralez. Fans chant for Jonny again, angering the big man further. European uppercuts by Moralez as he is in full control of this match, Storm catches a big boot by Moralez and charges and connects with a cross body, Storm attempts another big move but is caught by Moralez in a tilt-a-whirl backbreaker for a two count.

Moralez rams his knee into Storm's back and locks in a headlock "Jonny" chants from the AWW crowd, Ref checks Storms arm (it drops once, twice but he manages to keep it up the third time), fans rally behind Storm.

Elbows to Moralez's gut by Storm but Moralez cuts him down again with a knee to stomach. Moralez illegally fish hooks Storm, followed by a leg choke Storm reaches the ropes, Moralez doesn't break the hold. "I have until 5, Ref!" he bellows. Storm fights back yet again and quickly hits a jump up hurricanrana and his patented knee to the head but the Enzuguri that follows misses Moralez, but Storm catches Moralez on the button with a superkick, both men are down so the Ref starts the count.

He reaches 8 before both men return to their feet once more, "Jonny" chants from the AWW fans, elbows and a backdrop Moralez attempts (but Storm flips out) into a wheelbarrow DDT. No! Moralez reverses that into a northern lights suplex, Tiger driver attempt by Moralez, Storm manages to escape but gets caught again and this time Moralez hits the Tiger driver 1, 2 no! Storm kicks out! Moralez berates the Ref yet again, Storm hits a wheelbarrow into a sunset flip 1, 2 and 3!

Fans clap Storm as he takes a seat in the crowd, Moralez is seething, the AWW crowd make pirate noises towards him (which doesn't help matters). Storm poses for the crowd as they chant "Jonny" Storm shows appreciation to them by clapping.

Match Time: 13 minutes

Winner: 'Wonderkid' Jonny Storm

That was a very good big man vs little man match. Moralez was extremely dominant and looked like a killer at points in this match, Storm's performance was valiant as he took a beating but kept coming back.

Moralez's growing anger towards the Refereeing was beginning to tell and it looked like it may have an impact on the outcome of the match and it sure did. The contest between the Referee and Moralez was won on this occasion by the Ref!

Desirable Danny D & #1 Contender 'Rockstar' Spud vs AWW Champion Carnage (c) & Potter

Fans cheer as Danny D makes his way to the ring. "Danny D/Sucks!" stereo chant starts, teases crowd before coming out in a dress! There was a 'Carnage fears interesting wrestling matches' sign from a fan in the audience.

"Introducing the #1 Contender and soon to be AWW Champion, Spud!" Fans boo Spud as he enters, so he threatens them. Fans chant for Potter as Danny D and Spud leave. Loud Carnage chants from the AWW fans.

Spud and Danny D leave as Carnage poses for the crowd with the AWW title, Carnage invites them back in the ring (they decline).

"Potter" chants again, he enters wearing a 'Potter 3:16' shirt. The fans are on their feet, Carnage pushes Potter up the turnbuckle to pose for the crowd. Potter checks Carnage for foreign objects, the real Referee then checks Potter, Danny D picks up a chair. Ref starts a 10 count because Danny D and Spud are refusing to wrestle, they make it in and out again on the count of 9, they finally return to the ring.

Spud starts out, Carnage is chomping at the bit to get his hands on Spud. "Carnage!" chants from the fans, Spud runs away from Carnage and tags in Danny D. "Danny's gonna kill you!" chant starts up!

Shoulder block by Danny D knocks down Carnage, Carnage fires back with a spinning heel kick knocking Danny D down. Carnage tags Potter in Danny D runs away into Spud's crotch and then tags in Spud. "Potter" chants once more. Potter tags in Carnage and once again Spud tags back out.

Carnage tags Potter, Potter and Spud square off, Spud berates Potter and pushes him inadvertently into Carnage. Potter tags in Carnage, who stands right behind Spud, Spud feels around and looks in horror as he turns to meet Carnage, Spud quickly tags in Danny D. Danny D chops Carnage to no effect, Carnage's chop drops Danny D, suplex on Danny D then Carnage calls for Potter and makes the tag. Potter chops Danny D and hurts his own hand! He then pushes Danny D down and when back on his feet Potter and Danny D exchange 'girly slaps', Danny D tags in Spud.

Spud hits a top rope axe handle for a two count, fans rally behind Potter, Spud dropkicks Potter's face. Spud spits at Carnage causing the Referee to be distracted allowing for a double team on Potter by Spud and Danny D. "Danny D" chants, Danny D responds with a powerslam and a number of elbow drops "Save your boy" Danny D shouts at Carnage distracting the Referee once more allowing for another double team. Three amigos by Danny D gain a two count, the fans chant Potters name again!

Danny D hits a couple of backbreakers and then tags in Spud, Spud knee drops Potter for another two count. Punches to Potter's head follow the fans chant "Potter," Spud locks in a chinlock. "Danny D for Champion!" chant starts up. Carnage spits at Spud. Camel clutch by Spud, and then he stands on Potter's head. Spud tags in Danny D, Danny D does 'The Crab' and then locks in the Boston Crab, Potter struggles to the ropes and while there Spud pulls his arms adding more pressure to the move. Elbow by Danny D who then tags out to Spud, Spud taunts Carnage and slaps Potter.

While on the floor Spud stamps on Potter's hands, "Let's go, Potter!" chant starts up, chinlock by Spud. Knees to Potter's groin, Potter needs the tag, Potter catches Spud's boot and spikes him with a DDT! Fans erupt! Both men down Ref starts the count... he reaches 8 before Potter finally tags in Carnage while Spud tags in Danny D.

Danny D attempts a cross body but gets caught and fall away slammed by Carnage. Carnage ascends the turnbuckle and hits a missile dropkick on Danny D, razor's edge into a backbreaker gains a two count (as Spud attacks Carnage to break up the pin).

This allows Danny D to low blow Carnage and hit his TKO 1, 2 no! Potter breaks up the count! Carnage-Bolt on Danny D, Carnage unselfishly tags in Potter who kicks Danny D to make sure he is beaten.

Potter takes off his shirt and hits the Potter's elbow 1, 2 and 3.

Match Time: 17 minutes

Winners: AWW Champion Carnage (c) & Potter

Aftermath:
The place erupts, Spud leaves. Potter dumps Danny D out of the ring, fans clap for Carnage and Potter. Spud returns and gets Carnage-Bolted for his troubles, Potter's elbow? Fans chant, "Potter's elbow," and he gladly obliges. Carnage stands over Spud with the AWW Championship. Carnage hands Potter the AWW Title and he poses with it, Potter and Carnage thank the fans for their support.

Wow! That was an electric atmosphere, who would have imagined that a Referee would be the star of the show! Good old school tag team match, the Carnage vs Spud dynamic was incredible and when they wrestle one on one at Aston University it should be a great match. Potter put in a pretty good performance for his first ever match, a great way to end the show.

Top to bottom the best AWW card I have ever seen, good to great matches on the card made for a superb night of wrestling action, Danny Devine and BBS put on a great technical wrestling match, Geraden and Tommy Gunn left the fans in awe with high flying skills.

My only complaint is the fact that only 72 fans saw this great wrestling card take place, but apart from that a tremendous night of wrestling and a show that made me proud to be a fan.

Match of the Night:
'The Metrosexual' Danny Devine vs British Born Steele

Norton British Wrestling

Date: Sunday 30th September 2007
Time: 3:30pm
Attendance: 84
Price: Adults £8, Children £5, Family £17.
Location: Sports Nottingham Arena, Meadow Lane, Nottingham, East Midlands.

Trainee Match

Gonza vs 'Bam Bam' Barton

Lock-up in the centre of the ring, the stronger Barton pushes Gonza off. Lock-up once again this time Gonza rolls through, Barton calls for a test of strength but changes hands when the lock-up is about to take place, Gonza quickly tires of this and rolls up Barton for a two count. Gonza hits a hiptoss but Barton comes back with a huge boot to the stomach and repeated stamps on the downed Gonza. While down Barton knee's Gonza in the back and shouts, "Stay down." Gonza won't and rallies again with a chop, elbow and an armdrag reversal out of a powerslam attempted by Barton.

Barton charges at Gonza (who lowers the top rope) sending Barton to the outside of the ring. Gonza follows but misses with a dive, Gonza attempts to get back in but Barton stamps on his hand, Gonza asks a female fan to kiss his hand, but instead of that a male fan slaps it away! Gonza finally gets back in the ring, pushing the middle rope into Barton's crotch (sending him to the outside). Gonza follows up with a rope flip and an apron hurricanrana, both men return to the ring Gonza attempts a flying head scissors but Barton skilfully reverses it into a backbreaker.

Suplex by Barton gains a two count from the Referee, Barton knees Gonza in the back again and slaps on a chinlock. "Ask him, Ref!" Barton bellows, fans clap for Gonza. Elbows to the stomach break the hold, Gonza follows up with a flying head scissors into a roll up pin for a two count. Gonza jumps at Barton, Barton's waiting and quickly nails a powerbomb 1, 2, Gonza kicks out. Barton berates the Ref. Elbows to Barton's face by Gonza, he then swings and misses and is caught with a back body drop for a two count.

Barton's frustration shows as he leaves the ring to throw a chair (earning him a First public warning from the Ref). Gonza takes advantage with a run up the ropes DDT! Kick to the stomach by Gonza into another jumping DTT for a two count only. Gonza ascends the turnbuckle and hits a senton bomb on Barton, both men down (Ref reaches a 5 count before) Gonza reaches over and covers Barton for the 1, 2 and 3.

Match Time: 9 minutes

Winner: Gonza

That was a pretty good match up, especially considering it was between two trainees of NBW. Back and forth match that could have gone either way.

Barton's temper got the best of him at points and that allowed Gonza to showcase his speed and agility.

Two good prospects for the future of Norton British Wrestling.

NBW 'Revenge' Show

Surf Digby vs Sir Thomas Chamberlain w/Co-members of the Capital City Cliq (Stixx & 'Bombay Dream' Ross Jordan)

Surf Digby makes his way to the ring (the fans clap), Sir Thomas Chamberlain enters with co-members of the Capital City Cliq ('Bombay Dream' Ross Jordan & Stixx). "Make some noise for Sir Thomas Chamberlain!" The fans do, by booing loudly.

Stixx takes the microphone of the Ring Announcer; "Introducing the man that is better than anyone in the back and on par with us, Sir Thomas Chamberlain."

A fan shouts out, "Don't forget to take your dressing gown off!" This causes Stixx & Jordan to start jawing with the crowd.

Lock-up by both men, Chamberlain rolls Digby off, a second lock-up allows Chamberlain to hiptoss Digby.

A third lock-up and Chamberlain once again gets the advantage with a powerslam. Digby fires back though with an armdrag, hiptoss and powerslam causing Chamberlain to hastily exit the ring. CCC shout, "He's jealous of Sir Thomas Chamberlain's lovely hair." Chamberlain pulls up his knee pads and slides back in the ring. Lock-up into a headlock by Digby followed by a shoulder block. Chamberlain fires back with a punch and boot to the gut and dumps Digby to the outside.

CCC give Digby a beat down and then throw him back in the ring. Chamberlain applies the armlock. CCC taunt the fans, crowd claps for Digby, Chamberlain nails a clothesline for a two count. Jordan holds Stixx back from the fans, Digby ducks the clothesline attempt only to be hit with a clothesline on the return and once again he is dumped out of the ring for a CCC beat down. CCC throw Digby into the ring once again, suplex by Chamberlain gains a two count.

Chamberlain applies an armbar but Digby fights out with punches to the gut, ducking a clothesline attempt by Chamberlain hitting a flying elbow, back elbow and powerslam in quick succession for a two count. Fans clap for Digby once again, backbreaker by Digby who shouts to the fans, "Go up!" motioning to the top rope. Whilst there Jordan sneakily (behind the Referee's back) pushes him off. Chamberlain takes advantage with a whip shoulder first into the turnbuckle and quickly locking on the armbar for the submission win.

Stixx takes the mic again "The winner of the match from the great city of London, Sir Thomas Chamberlain" the fans boo the Capital City Cliq as they leave.

Match Time: 7 minutes

Winner: Sir Thomas Chamberlain w/Co-members of the Capital City Cliq (Stixx & 'Bombay Dream' Ross Jordan)

Pretty solid match to start the main show off with. Back and forth match between the two competitors,

Digby may have had the match won but the constant interference by Stixx and 'Bombay Dream' Ross Jordan proved too much for him to overcome in the end. Chamberlain's offence was pretty sound working constantly on Digby's arm (the same arm) that made Digby submit.

> For #1 Contendership to either the NBW Cruiserweight (if Travis wins) and Middleweight Championship (if Dragon wins)

> 'Shooting Star' Kris Travis vs Imperial Dragon

Fans boo Travis as he makes his way to the ring, Travis pushes the Referee out of the way and poses for the crowd. Fans clap for Imperial Dragon (who slaps hands with the crowd) on his way to the ring. Travis shouts for the Ref, "Check his damn tassels." Dragon shouts, "Come on people!" the fans respond by cheering loudly.

Lock-up in the centre of the ring, Dragon pushes Travis back into the corner. He accuses Dragon of a hair pull (even though he was pulling Dragon's hair, unbeknownst to the Ref). Boot to the stomach by Travis, who quickly applies the headlock to Dragon. Dragon reverses out and hits a shoulder block, Dragon leapfrogs Travis and hits a roll through armdrag, Travis returns with a Japanese armdrag, Travis misses a punch and is rammed into the corner by Dragon, Travis then bellows for the Ref to "Get him back."

Armdrag by Dragon, followed up by a hiptoss and chop in seamless fashion. Back body drop by Dragon, Travis rolls to the outside, Dragon attempts a suicide dive but Travis kicks him square in the head! Travis rolls back in and returns with a chop to Dragon, Travis Irish whips Dragon but he reverses it and follows with a high knee strike to Travis's head. Dragon calls for a 10 punch in the corner, he reaches 9 before he is pushed off and into a big boot by Travis for a two count.

Travis follows up with a boot to Dragon's head, snapmere and a kick to the back for another two count. Travis berates the Ref, he then returns to pull Dragon's hair (Ref reaches a 3 count), suplex by Travis gains a two count (as Dragon's foot was on the ropes). Another snapmere by Travis this time into a headlock "Ask him Ref" he shouts, fans clap for Dragon. Dragon fights back, ducking a clothesline attempt by Travis and hitting an Enzuguri and Blue thunder driver for a two count. Dragon motions for the elbow, but his attempt misses Travis, who hits with an Enzuguri to the back of Dragon's head.

Rolling suplex by Travis follows. Travis pushes the Ref out of the way (for that he gets his First public warning), Travis puts Dragon on top rope and poses for the crowd, punches by Dragon and a front suplex drop Travis to the mat. Missile dropkick by Dragon, who then nips up, hitting a forearm and monkey flip in quick succession, and even a Michinoku driver for a close nearfall. "Come on" he shouts to the fans, which causes the fans to clap once more. Travis pulls Dragon's tights throwing him towards the Ref, Dragon and the Ref don't collide but it distracts Dragon and allows Travis to hit a Jay Driller for the 1, 2 and 3.

Ring Announcer announces that 'Shooting Star' Kris Travis is the NEW #1 Contender to El Ligero's NBW Cruiserweight Championship.

Match Time: 10 minutes

Winner and NEW #1 Contender to El Ligero's NBW Cruiserweight Championship: 'Shooting Star' Kris Travis

Both men were evenly matched against each other and this provided a very good match for the NBW fans. Dragon had his chances to win the match as did Travis, in the end the cheating tactics that Travis used for most of the match paid off for him. Ligero vs Travis should be a very good match in its own right and one that I look forward to seeing when it takes place.

> Stephanie Scope w/Co-members of The
> Establishment ('Textbook' Dave Frazier &
> 'Malicious' Paul Malen) vs Roxi

The NBW fans boo The Establishment as they make their way to the ring, "You're not allowed to boo a Champion," Dave Frazier replies. Roxi is cheered as she makes her way to the ring (slapping hands with the fans) as she does. The Referee decides to ban The Establishment from ringside causing the fans to chant "Out" at them, they begrudgingly leave.

Scope attacks Roxi from behind, Roxi returns with a clothesline and shouts "Easy, Easy." Scope leaves the ring and after a few seconds Roxi leaves also and the chase is on. Both women return to the ring, Roxi runs at the ropes causing both women to criss cross the ring, Roxi points for Scope to look up and then slaps her across the face. Scope decides to start another criss cross but when she points for Roxi to look up, Roxi stamps on her toes. Roxi then attempts to knock Scope down with a three shoulder blocks but she can't move the stronger woman that is until she attempts and connects with a fourth.

Scope quickly returns with a clothesline knocking Roxi down. Scope hits Roxi with a number of boots to the back and then chokes her in the ropes, shouting "Yeah" the fans reply by booing. Hairtoss follows and another choke with the boot, Scope uses her full 5 count. Snapmere on Roxi followed by Scope standing on Roxi's hair while pulling her arms, Scope does the same again but on the third attempt Roxi rolls her up and almost gains the pinfall. Roxi quickly follows up with a backslide for a two count.

Scope returns with a kick to the back of Roxi's legs, tosses her by the hair and chokes with her boot in the ropes before pulling Roxi away and gaining a two count. Scope places her leg over Roxi's throat while asking the Ref about a slow count (unbeknownst to the Ref she was choking Roxi with her leg and boot). Scope applies an armlock and while the Ref isn't looking pulls on Roxi's hair with her free hand, the Ref checks for a hair pull (so Scope bites on Roxi's hand), Roxi is somehow able to roll through for a pin but only manages a two count.

Roxi rolls under a Scope clothesline, hitting a knee to Scope's stomach and nailing her with a neck breaker (fans clap for Roxi). The Ref counts both women down (he reaches 9 before they return to their feet). Both women trade forearms, Dave Frazier hides at ringside, Roxi hit's a DDT for a two count (fans clap for Roxi again). Roxi runs at the ropes and is tripped by Frazier, Frazier gets on apron to distract Roxi but collides with Scope allowing Roxi to roll her up and get the 1, 2 and 3.

"Roxi!" chants from the fans as The Establishment argue (Scope leaves) as the fans clap once more for Roxi.

Match Time: 8 minutes

Winner: Roxi

Good back and forth match between two of the premier wrestlers on the women's wrestling scene in the U.K. The match could have gone either way with both women having chances to end it, interference backfired for the first time of the night and Roxi managed to pull out the win. Cracks are appearing in The Establishment, will it fall apart at the seams?

NBW Tag Team Titles

Capital City Cliq (Ross Jordan & Stixx) vs Killer Instinct (Tiger X & Angelblade) (c)

The Capital City Cliq are booed as they make their way to the ring. Stixx once again steals the microphone away from the Ring Announcer. "I do the damn announcing! Introducing 'Bombay Dream' Ross Jordan and Heavyweight 'Master of Pain' Stixx, we're going to take the NBW Tag Belts back to London." Killer Instinct make their way to ringside with the fans cheers ringing in their ears (slapping fans hands on the way).

CCC attack from behind, Killer Instinct reverse with a double dropkick knocking Stixx to the outside, they also knock Jordan to the outside with a double dropkick. "London sucks!" chants by the NBW fans. Angelblade grabs Stixx by the ears, Stixx drops Blade on the ropes and re-enters the ring. Blade returns with a leg lariat and tags out to Tiger X. Double hiptoss by Killer Instinct and a splash/leg drop combination quickly follow. Stixx rakes X's eyes and tags out to Jordan.

Hiptoss and a backbreaker/leg drop combination on Jordan by Killer Instinct. Jordan reverses X's Irish whip but with a possible double team coming X ducks and Stixx clotheslines his own partner (fans clap for Killer Instinct). Jordan reverses another Irish whip attempt into the waiting Stixx who trips X, knee to the back by Jordan and an eye rake follow "Make some noise" shouts Blade (fans clap once again). Elbows and a neck snap by Jordan for a two count Jordan questions "Biased, Ref?" Boot to the head downs X again, now he asks for support from the crowd.

Tag into Blade, Jordan's forearm knocks Blade down Jordan asks the Ref, "Check the kneepads!" The Ref does as instructed, this allows Jordan to choke Blade.

"London sucks!" chant the fans once more. "London doesn't suck," Jordan replies (fans clap for Angelblade). Irish whip by Blade, big boot and a powerslam follow for a two count. Jordan tags in Stixx, who quickly knocks X off the apron. "Baldy!" chants from the crowd. Stixx applies the Abdominal stretch, (with the Ref distracted by X trying to get in the ring) Stixx slaps his hands together (Ref hears a legal tag).

Stixx grabs Jordan's arm to add more leverage to the Abdominal stretch and spits at Tiger X. Blind tag again behind the Referee's back and Stixx applies another Abdominal stretch this time Blade reverses into a hiptoss and both men fall to the canvas causing the Referee to start a 10 count. Jordan flies off the top rope with an axe handle to Blade, Stixx knees Blade in the back and applies the chinlock whilst pulling Blade's hair. Fans clap for Blade once more, Stixx knees Blade in the stomach and then tags in Jordan who poses for the crowd chanting, "London rules!" to which the fans reply, "London sucks!"

Blade escapes and pushes Jordan down for a quick two count. Double clothesline and both men are down so the Ref starts the count, Jordan is up and quickly attacks X. Blade shoulder blocks Jordan and finally tags in X, X quickly hits a TKO on Jordan and a T-Bone suplex on Stixx. X misses a clothesline on Stixx and is hoisted onto his shoulders for what looks like a doomsday device, Jordan misses the top rope clothesline as X counters with a victory roll for a two count.

Stixx eye rakes X and dumps him out of the ring, Stixx whips Blade into the turnbuckle but misses with the follow up and gets caught with a backcracker. Jordan kicks Blade and connects with a jumping neckbreaker, Stixx follows up with a clothesline then shouts "London" (the fans boo loudly). Jordan attempts a clothesline but the returning X ducks sending Jordan to the outside. Double gorilla press slam by Killer Instinct on Stixx

1, 2 Jordan pulls the Ref out feigning injury, Chamberlain runs down to ringside to attack (but is foiled) as Stixx is pushed off the top rope, X follows with a frog splash.

Jordan rams Blade into the steel ringpost, Chamberlain hands Stixx a weapon (which he places on his hand). Stixx punches X directly in the face for the 1, 2 and 3! The fans boo the CCC and clap and cheer for Killer Instinct on their exit from the ring.

Match Time: 14 minutes

Winners and NEW NBW Tag Team Champions: Capital City Clique (Ross Jordan & Stixx) (c)

That was a very good old school tag team match. Good wrestling from both teams, CCC using every advantage they could get legal or otherwise, Killer Instinct putting in a good, valiant but ultimately losing performance. With the way the match ended (Chamberlain's interference) I would say a rematch is on the cards and that is a rematch that I would welcome.

INTERMISSION

Patriot Games Gauntlet Match

Abdullah Quadir's Foreign Fanatics vs Jay Techno's English Army

The Foreign Fanatics are booed by the partisan English crowd as they make their way to the ring, The English Army are cheered by the NBW fans.

Techno takes the microphone. "I'm sick of you guys disrespecting our country," and asks the fans to stand for the English national anthem. Fans throw bits of paper at the Foreign Fanatics. Fans clap loudly during the English national anthem and chant, "England!" Before the match Quadir rips down the England flag on the wall and replaces it with the Moroccan flag.

Nirus and Frenchman Mark Mignot start the match, Nitrus stretches Mignot, he ducks under the resulting clothesline attempt and dropkicks Mignot (after ducking a couple of clothesline attempts). Mignot fights back with a snapmere and rakes Nitrus's eyes with his boot, and repeatedly stamps on Nitrus's hands. "Nitrus!" chants from the fans. Nitrus fires back with forearms on Mignot, Mignot turns the tables with a choke using his boot, and a tree of woe which he uses to choke Nitrus once more.

Fans clap and chant "Come on England," Irish whip by Nitrus leads to a back body drop on Mignot. Mignot is dumped over the ropes, Mignot is then rolled back in to the ring, Nitrus connects with a victory roll by but Mignot reverses and with his feet on the ropes gets the 1, 2 and 3.

Nitrus of the English Army has been eliminated after 4 minutes of the match.

Adrenaline has ascended the top rope, he connects with a high cross body on Mignot for the 1, 2 and 3.

Mark Mignot of the Foreign Fanatics has been eliminated after 4 minutes 5 seconds of the match.

Mignot and 'Tinseltown' Sebastian Pedin double team Adrenaline for a one count. Hurricanrana by Adrenaline but Pedin quickly applies a backbreaker, Pedin then distracts the Ref (allowing Casey to illegally choke Adrenaline). He then takes off

Adrenaline's England top and spits on it! The fans chant, "England!" another backbreaker by Pedin for a two count. Irish whip clothesline is ducked and Adrenaline hits a springboard knee to Pedin's face.

Both men are down, Ref starts the count and reaches 8 before both men return to their feet trading forearms as they do. Pedin catches Adrenaline and powerslams him, he then goes up top but misses with an attempted tumbling splash, Adrenaline hits a moonsault and a twisting senton for the 1, 2 and 3.

'Tinseltown' Sebastian Pedin of the Foreign Fanatics has been eliminated after 8 minutes.

'Special Edition' Joseph Conners attacks Adrenaline and quickly puts him away with a fall away DDT for the 1, 2 and 3.

Adrenaline of the English Army has been eliminated after 8 minutes 15 seconds.

Chebby chops Conners and whips him into the turnbuckle, Chebby misses with a moonsault kick and is caught in Conners' fall away DDT for the 1, 2 and 3.

Chebby of the English Army has been eliminated after 9 minutes 5 seconds.

"England!" chants once again from the NBW fans. English Army's Team Captain Jay Techno enters, he ducks an attempted clothesline and hits Conners with a dropkick, an armdrag, drop toe hold and seamlessly into a cradle for a two count. Backslide gets another two count, Crucifix into a sunset flip for another nearfall by Techno. Conners returns with a Russian legsweep. "You're rubbish!" shouts a fan. "Shut your mouth," Conners replies. Necksnap by Conners followed up with a leg drop for a two count.

Choke on the ropes (fans clap for Techno), Conners whips Techno face first into the turnbuckle and pins him again for another two count. Another choke with the boot as the Foreign Fanatics distract the Ref, backbreaker by Conners but his nonchalant cover doesn't get the job done "Told you to pay the Ref off" he shouts at Quadir.

"Come on England!" chants by the crowd, Techno's double boot catches Conners as he runs in, he quickly follows up with a top rope bulldog for a two count. Forearms are traded by both men, eye rake by Conners, following up with his fall away DDT but no! Techno reverses into a roll up pin for the 1, 2 and 3.

'Special Edition' Joseph Conners of the Foreign Fanatics has been eliminated after 14 minutes.

Conners isn't done with Techno, attacking him from behind with the fall away DDT, he then takes the microphone "I don't care about Foreigners or English, the only person I care about is myself!" Fans clap for Techno, Quadir chokes Techno and repeatedly stamps on him, he climbs up to the top rope and hits an axe handle for a two count. Punch to the ribs and a boot by Quadir, Tiger driver attempted and connects but Techno kicks out at two!

Quadir attempts another Tiger driver but this time Techno rolls through and gets the 1, 2 and 3. Fans clap and cheer as the rest of the English Army make their way back down to ringside to celebrate, fans throw rubbish at Quadir and chant "Loser" at him.

Abdullah Quadir of the Foreign Fanatics has been eliminated after 18 minutes.

Match Time: 18 minutes

Winners: Jay Techno and the English Army

That was a tremendous concept put forth by Norton British Wrestling, as there was no divide. The NBW fans hated the Foreign Fanatics and loved the English Army leading to a series of football like chants which created a tremendous atmosphere. The match though was rushed at some points (which is understandable with a 20 minute time limit).

A few quick pinfalls which created can't miss action but also because of its very nature created a blink and you might miss it match. That's not to say it wasn't a good match but I feel it would have benefited from a 25 or maybe 30 minute time limit.

Street Fight

NBW Heavyweight Title

'Malicious' Paul Malen w/'Textbook' Dave Frazier vs 'Playboy' Phil Bedwell (c)

Malen is booed as he makes his way to ringside, Bedwell is cheered as makes his way to ringside.

Bedwell rushes the ring and the two competitors fight even before the bell has rung! Bedwell clotheslines Malen over the top rope to the ringside floor, Malen is annoyed and throws a chair towards Frazier. Malen returns to the ring and quickly clubs Bedwell on the back, and chokes him with his boot (forcing Bedwell to the outside). Bedwell is attacked on the outside by Frazier, Malen forearms him off the apron, Bedwell trips up Malen and brings him out of the ring. Bedwell powerslams Malen and rams his head off the ring apron, a chop to the chest follows as does a plastic chair to Malen's back.

Malen fights back with a kick to the stomach (the fans clap for Bedwell) and headbutts Bedwell directly in the head.

Malen continues the attack with a leather belt to the back and a choke with a ringside chair, the second time Bedwell blocks and suplexes Malen on the floor (as the fans clap for Bedwell once more). Frazier asks Malen, "How much do you want it?" Bedwell connects with a dropkick through the ropes, but is smacked with a steel sheet to the head on the second attempt. Malen chokes Bedwell with his hand and then his boot, while Frazier jaws with the NBW fans, Malen hits Bedwell with the steel sheet to the head once again.

Bedwell fights back with a chinbreaker causing Malen to ask Frazier for a belt. Hilariously Frazier asks back, "Which one?" (as there are three belts at ringside). Frazier decides on the leather one and hands it to Malen who uses it to choke Bedwell, Frazier then chokes Bedwell with the belt. Malen exits the ring and returns with a steel chain which he uses to choke Bedwell with once again, Frazier turns to the fans "Take a nice picture" Malen continues the assault with a club to Bedwell's neck, Malen rings Bedwell's bell (literally) and rams him into the steelpost.

The fans aren't happy. Malen tells them, "You need to shut your mouth!" Bedwell tries to rally with a piledriver but it's reversed into a back body drop on the floor. "Make him bleed!" Frazier shouts. Malen poses with the NBW Title (as the fans clap for

Bedwell). Malen sets up a steel chair in the ring and shouts, "Have a seat, Phil!" sarcastically. Bedwell reverses Malen into a drop toe hold which causes Malen to connect head first with the chair. Malen low blows Bedwell and uses the chair on Bedwell's back, ribs and head in quick succession but only manages a two count.

Fans clap for Bedwell. Frazier shouts, "Stop clapping!" Cobra clutch by Malen, Bedwell fights out with elbows to the gut only to be caught with a knee to the stomach. Malen poses allowing Bedwell to hit a DDT. Powerslam by Bedwell, knee to the lower back and a sideslam for a two count. Bedwell climbs to the top rope and hits a flying forearm. "Yeah," he shouts. Bedwell grabs the chair (whilst Malen grabs a Singapore cane), Malen connects with the cane to Bedwell's stomach and then chokes him with it.

"I'll get a table!" he bellows and brings a table into the ring, he then returns to Bedwell cracking the cane over his back and throws Bedwell back into the ring. Headbutts by Malen, rapid punches (fans clap for Bedwell) chop, and a punch. Bedwell fights back with punches of his own, powerbomb by Bedwell through the table and both men are down. There is a look of disbelief on Frazier's face, Bedwell follows up with a low blow and smacks the chair into Malen's back and head screaming, "Yeah and over."

Frazier gets up on the apron so Bedwell slingshots Malen at Frazier, and quickly follows with a jumping piledriver on the chair for the 1, 2 and 3. The fans cheer for Bedwell, Malen is bloodied and bruised, Frazier berates Malen. Malen attempts to attack Frazier but he squirms away into Bedwell's hands and he too is piledriven for his troubles to a loud cheer from the NBW fans! Fans clap loudly for Bedwell as Malen walks out on Frazier.

Match Time: 19 minutes

Winner and STILL NBW Heavyweight Champion: 'Playboy' Phil Bedwell (c)

Whoa! That was an intense match, a truly great way to end the show. You could feel the hatred between the two competitors and once again the fans loved Bedwell and hated Malen. Frazier was hilarious at ringside jawing with the fans, the action was back and forth as well and like a lot of the other matches on the show could have gone either way. I wouldn't mind a rematch but I think the big issue is how long before The Establishment falls apart completely.

My first time at Norton British Wrestling and I enjoyed a good afternoon of Wrestling action, the Trainee match surpassed my expectations, all the matches were filled with solid wrestling, Roxi and Scope produced a good women's match, the NBW Tag Team Titles match was a good old school tag match, the Patriot games gauntlet match was a lot of fun albeit a little rushed and the main event was intense and produced a very good match in its own right. My only complaint is for the ring announcing, which was very difficult to hear throughout the afternoon.

Match of the Night:
Street Fight – NBW Heavyweight Title
'Malicious' Paul Malen with 'Textbook' Dave Frazier vs 'Playboy' Phil Bedwell (c)

September 2007 Thoughts

My Live Match of September 2007:
Zack Sabre Jr vs Chris Stone vs Ashton Smith vs Stiro (Triple X 'Jak'ed up' 9th September 2007)

My Live Show of September 2007:
Anti-Watershed Wrestling (27th September 2007)

11. OCTOBER 2007

Triple X Wrestling

Date: Sunday 7th October 2007
Time: 4:00pm
Attendance: 60
Price: £7
Location: Jumping Jaks, Coventry Skydome, Coventry, West Midlands.

Gabriel Grey is your Ring Announcer for this evening.

"If you want me to start the show, play my music," Grey shouts, whilst in the ring the fans jeer loudly. "Don't boo me because at the end of the day, I'm awesome!" Grey retorts.

'Mr Bad Attitude' Martin Kirby vs Trip-El Ligero

Hilarious opening match, El Ligero became Trip-El Ligero (pretending he was Triple H). Ligero's Triple H mannerisms were spot on! Kirby's girlish screams also added a lot of comedy to the match.

After all the comedy a pretty good match took place, with back and forth action between the two competitors.

Funny moment when Ligero hit Kirby with a spinebuster (Ligero went down like he had blown his quadriceps muscle!).

Ligero's numerous attempts at the Pedigree, finally paid off in the end as a setup to Ligero's finishing move the springboard into a DDT (C4L) for the 1, 2 and 3.

Match Time: 12 minutes

Winner: Trip-El Ligero

Fun way to start the show!

> Icons of Dominance (John Bull & Scott Grimm w/The Boss) & Omer Ibrahim vs Sidekicks (CK Light & 'That 70's' Andy Shoes) & 'E-Train' Edgar Stryfe

Good tag team action and the atmosphere surrounding it created an enjoyable match. Omer wasn't really a team player though even almost showing the Referee Bull and Grimm cheating. Omer finally had enough and gored both Bull and Grimm before leaving the ring, leaving CK, Shoes and Stryfe with a 3 on 2 advantage or so they thought.

Stryfe out of nowhere attacked both Shoes and Light forcing the Referee to throw the match out. Stryfe made his feelings know directly after the match "I'm always stuck in these tag team matches."

Match Time: 14 minutes

Winners: No Contest

Stryfe turning his back on Light and Shoes came out of nowhere and produced a wow, did that really just happen moment.

Zack Sabre Jr vs Chris Stone

This match was as brutal as it was tremendous! Sabre's kicks were just incredibly brutal and at points you had to kind of feel bad for Stone. Sabre showed his entire repertoire of submission moves and the different ways of applying such holds (even at one point standing on Stone's face when he was locked in an armbar).

Stone fought back though and went toe to toe with Sabre once more, even managing to hit A Stone's Throw (his Finishing move) for a nearfall. Sabre's offence was mostly centred around Stone's arm, that played heavily in the finale of this match with Sabre rolling through an attempted electric chair drop straight into the hyper extension of Stone's arm which caused the tap out.

Match Time: 17 minutes

Winner: Zack Sabre Jr

The match that I paid £7 to witness live, lived up to my expectations as both wrestlers put forth an outstanding contest that was well worth the price of admission alone.

Cameron Kraze vs Devilman

This was another match with a lot of comedy moments, Devilman was the clear favourite of the fans (with numerous "Devil-man" chants). The action was back and forth in this match also, with Kraze using underhand tactics to his advantage and Devilman using his chopping ability (especially to the face) to reverse his fortunes in the match.

Devilman had a little too much for Kraze in the end and finished the match with a Hurricane DDT and a Brainbuster for the 3 count. Much to the delight of the Triple X fans!

Match Time: 11 minutes

Winner: Devilman

Jimmy Havoc vs Anonymity vs Shelf

After losing to Jon Ryan at the last show Havoc wanted to prove something to himself, and was set up against an unknown opponent (which happened to be a wrestler called Anonymity). Havoc brought Shelf to the ring with him and the Referee turned the match into a triple threat featuring Havoc, Anonymity and Shelf! (Yes an in adamant object was a competitor in a wrestling match). The Triple X fans chants for "Shelf" were almost deafening, as the match was taking place. Havoc and Anonymity wrestled a quick paced match as Shelf looked on, Shelf even managed to get a nearfall!

After being dominated in the early going Anonymity fought back and looked scheduled to gain the upset win. At this point he left the ring and returned with two wooden chairs which he set up Shelf on, this allowed Havoc too much time and on the second attempt he gorilla press slammed Anonymity through Shelf and the chairs and with a DVD later picked up the win. What I'm about to say may shock you… but an in adamant object was the biggest star on the entire card!

Match Time: 5 minutes

Winner: Jimmy Havoc

Ashton Smith vs Spud

The Triple X fans are fully behind Ashton. Spud controlled the early going, with Ashton only seemingly having a glimmer of a chance at winning the match, Spud made a costly mistake mid-match and all of a sudden was on the back foot. At this point Spud leaves the ring and calls for a rock-off! Spud's air guitar only raised crowd apathy while Ashton's dancing wowed the crowd.

The rock-off only posed as a distraction though as Spud attacked Ashton from behind regaining the advantage. The match began turning in Ashton's favour once more (as he looked for that elusive win in Triple X) and just as he had the match won, Spud rolled his leather belt around his hand and clocked Ashton with it winning the match.

Match Time: 15 minutes

Winner: Spud

Winner of Rock-Off: Ashton

Another match that I thought had a lot of potential turned into a good match and with the ending, Ashton vs Spud 2 looks to be on the cards and I'm all for that.

Damned Nation (Dragon Aisu & Majik w/Gabriel Grey) vs Jexodus (Jekkel & Exodus)

Aisu walks over to me and steals my notebook away! Reading while he sits in the corner awaiting his opponents (he's obviously a fan! Well that's what I'd like to think). Fans are fully behind Jexodus. Jexodus control the early going of the match, with numerous quick tags cutting off the ring from their opponents. This all changes when Exodus is whipped into the ropes where Aisu is (Aisu trips and hangs Exodus on the ropes) allowing Majik to take over. Majik and Aisu take it in turns to rile up the crowd. "Clap your hands if you're a retard!" followed by numerous chinlocks at different points in the match (much to the crowd's chagrin).

Aisu and Majik look all set for the win but by this point they have made Exodus mad and he suddenly fights back and shows no ill effects to Aisu's half nelson suplex! Exodus finally makes the tag to Jekkel and the match is swinging Jexodus's way, Jekkel ascends the turnbuckle but Grey stops him, Jekkel then chases after Grey leaving Exodus alone with the Damned Nation. Exodus fights but is soon finished off with an elevated Flatliner by Majik for the 3 count.

Match Time: 11 minutes

Winners: Damned Nation (Dragon Aisu & Majik w/Gabriel Grey)

Good way to end the show, this feud has been building up for a few months in Triple X and once again with how it ended I believe a rematch maybe in the pipeline and that is just fine by me.

Top to bottom another good show by Triple X, a lot of different styles meshed together and they worked well. Comedy (numerous hilarious moments during the show highlighted by Trip-El Ligero), Atmosphere (numerous creative chants by the Triple X crowd), great wrestling action (Chris Stone vs Zack Sabre Jr) a truly shocking moment when Edgar Stryfe turned his back on CK Light and Andy Shoes.

A rock off and the hottest rising star in Triple X Wrestling - Shelf! This is the kind of show that should be seen by far more than 60 fans! Although Triple X is seen as being for an acquired taste if you're looking for good wrestling from top to bottom I say you should give Triple X a go.

Match of the Night:
Zack Sabre Jr vs Chris Stone

Legends Wrestling League
(LWL Aftershock Report Part 2)

Date: Tuesday 9th October 2007
Time: 7:30pm
Attendance: 52
Price: Adults £5, £4 with LWL Flyer (Downloadable from http://www.lwluk.co.uk) Kids £3
Location: Legends Members Club, Oxley Street, Wolverhampton, West Midlands.

Motor Mouth Mike is once again your Ring Announcer for the evening.

Platinum Paul Paige vs Chandler Scott Lee

Paige controls the early going, showing superior wrestling ability to his opponent and the LWL fans. CSL is able to fight his way back into the match, but every time he looks like he has a clear advantage Paige would reach the ropes or leave the ring. The fans let Paige know exactly what they thought of his legal but cowardly tactics, one fan shouted "Give him a dummy" much to the audiences pleasure. Paige and CSL went toe to toe once more in a pretty even contest.

The fans took a little while to get fully into the match. That was until CSL was fading from Paige's sleeper hold, when CSL managed to keep his hand up when it looked like falling for the third time the fans let out a huge scream! The contest continued evenly until Paige went for the Impaler, with CSL reversing out and gaining control of the match. Paige pulled the Referee in the way and low blow-ed CSL before quickly hitting the Impaler for the 1, 2 and 3.

Match Time: 19 minutes

Winner: Platinum Paul Paige

Too long for an opening match but it was a decent effort put forth from the two competitors.

Sykes vs Kris Navarro

Sykes did a lot not to endear himself to the crowd. "Any crap from any of you lot and I'll slap each and every one of you!" Whilst squaring off with his opponent Navarro: "You look like an extra out of mallrats."

Sykes and Navarro trade holds in the early going, when Navarro got the advantage Sykes slipped out of the ring. Threatening a fan, "Unlike a lot of these guys I don't make false promises, I'll rip your face off!" Sykes is not a fan of the Legends Members Club's beer either! Sykes littered the match with cheap underhand tactics behind the Referee's back (twisting Navarro's fingers when he was supposed to have a wristlock on, etc). Sykes once again showed apathy towards the LWL crowd; "This is a safety net, granddad," when a fan questions his continual escaping of moves via the ropes.

Sykes frustration grew as no matter what he did he couldn't put away the resilient Navarro, even with his continual use of underhand tactics Navarro just wouldn't stay down! Sykes hit an armcracker but that only managed a two count. Sykes's anger grew and grew. "Told you not to piss me off!" he shouts at Navarro, Navarro and Sykes traded punches leading the LWL crowd into duelling chants of, "Whey/Boo!" The underhand tactics continued as Sykes debuted the finger rake on the ropes (a move which I had never seen before), Navarro fought back with a hurricanrana and a huge spear for an incredibly close nearfall.

Then after his inability to put Navarro away Sykes finally snapped and with Navarro on the mat unleashed a barrage of forearms when the ref started the count Sykes refused to break at 5 which caused the Disqualification. Sykes wasn't done though as he continued the assault and finished off by hitting an armcracker before leaving.

Match Time: 13 minutes

Winner by Disqualification: Kris Navarro

That was a truly superb match from bell to bell, a debut that Sykes should be proud of and a performance Navarro should be equally proud of! Great wrestling, crowd atmosphere and even with a DQ finish it made sense (because of Sykes growing anger). It didn't take away from the match at all. With the DQ finish it looks like LWL is heading for Sykes vs Navarro 2, I would love to see that match!

LWL National Pride Championship

Dan Ryder vs Johnny 'The Body' Costello (c)

Costello refuses to wrestle until Motor Mouth Mike says his introduction in an American accent, drawing a lot of boos from the LWL fans. Ryder was met with loud cheers on his entrance followed by "England" chants. Costello has trouble getting into the ring and hilariously trips himself up on the rope, falling flat on his face.

The match starts pretty evenly but when Costello gets a slight advantage he acts like he has the match won "I'm the champion." Ryder and Costello have a somersault competition (Ryder wins) but Costello's attempt and subsequent crotching of himself on the middle turnbuckle was incredibly funny. Ryder attempted to follow up so Costello dropped to his knees and crotched himself on the steel ringpost! The match regains some normalcy as Ryder and Costello trade holds, Costello shouts: "I'm the champ-ionone."

Ryder uses this to his advantage hitting his patented standing moonsault for a two count. Ryder attempts to get the big man down with shoulder blocks but he isn't powerful enough, so Ryder hits a sunset flip even pulling down Costello's tights!

Costello continues with his ass hanging out (much to displeasure of the fans in the crowd), Ryder executes a drop toe hold on the ropes. "6-1-9!" he shouts but Costello rolls out and comes back with a 6-1-9 attempt of his own but instead of executing the move he exits the ring and kicks Ryder in the head.

"I'm gonna break his damn back!" Costello shouts as he attacks Ryder's back, Ryder reverses out and hits a bulldog quickly following up with a picture perfect 450 splash for the 1, 2 and 3. LWL has a NEW National Pride Champion and his name is Dan Ryder!

Match Time: 11 minutes

Winner and NEW LWL National Pride Champion: Dan Ryder (c)

Incredibly funny comedy match put forth by the two competitors, creative chanting from the LWL crowd created a tremendous atmosphere.

INTERMISSION

Mad Dog Maxx vs 'Sik' Nik Dutt

Maxx gets a "We're not worthy!" chant from the LWL faithful as he enters to which he replies, "Shut your stinking mouths!" which causes the fans to strangely clap for Maxx! Dutt gets cheered as he makes his way to the ring, but the fans are definitely split with "Let's go Nik/Let's go Mad Dog" duelling chants. Mad Dog gets the better of the early going and shows his complete disrespect for Dutt by spitting in his face. This had a positive reaction for Dutt because he came out firing on all cylinders with slaps and chops putting Mad Dog on the back foot. Fans started to turn more towards Dutt with chants of "Mad Dog sucks!" to which Mad Dog replied, "SHUT UP!"

Mad Dog then takes the match to the outside as the two wrestlers brawl around the ringside area, with that Mad Dog has control of the match. Mad Dog would gain further control of the match by using legal but still slightly cowardly tactics (choking Dutt as he was in the ropes until the Ref counted to 4). Still Mad Dog couldn't put Dutt away, even after hitting a turnbuckle neckbreaker and dropkick on Dutt whilst he was in the tree of woe.

Dutt fought back and with an elevated facebuster gained a close nearfall, Dutt continued the offence with a jumping slice bread #2 for another two count. As the fans were clapping for Dutt he motioned for the superkick. Maxx managed to catch Dutt's boot and spun him around into a pulling piledriver for the 1, 2 and 3 count.

Match Time: 17 minutes

Winner: Mad Dog Maxx

Good match, Dutt looked competitive in losing as it was a back and forth contest for the majority of the match. Maxx put forth a good performance also and really in terms of fan endearment both men were winners.

LWL Championship

'The Metro-Sexual' Danny Devine vs Mat Mensa (c)

Motor Mouth Mike does his best Bruce Buffer impression: "Let's get ready to ruuuuuuuuuumble!" Devine enters to boos from the crowd. Devine continues spraying fans with deodorant as he walks, Mensa comes down to the ring to loud cheers. Mensa poses with the LWL Heavyweight Belt on the turnbuckle allowing Devine to attack from behind, sending Mensa sprawling to the outside.

Devine picks up a chair and swings at Mensa's head and ringpost, luckily for Mensa, Devine hits just the ringpost. Mensa and Devine brawl around ringside with Mensa getting the better of the exchange. Mensa awkwardly flunk his arm at Devine but then cleverly changed into a sleeper hold, before following up with a suplex for a two count. Devine counters a second suplex and hit's the Rude awakening (complete with hip gyration) for a two count of his own.

Devine shouts, "Metro!" he misses a splash in the corner (crotching himself on the middle turnbuckle), Mensa quickly follows up with a stalling suplex but can only manage another 2 count. Fans clap for Mensa as both men struggle back to their feet, trading punches, Devine gets the better of this exchange and quickly locks in the camel clutch. "I'm going to break his neck just for you," he shouts, pointing at a fan. Crowd chants for Mensa once more. "Let's go, Mensa, let's go," Mensa powers out!

A drop toe hold stops Mensa in his tracks and dumps him to outside of the ring, Devine quickly follows up with a running clothesline off the apron. Devine shouts "Metro-Sexual baby!" He then drinks a fans energy drink, this allows Mensa back in the match and he gorilla press slams Devine on the table in front of me. The fans chant "This is awesome." Mensa throws Devine back in the ring, Devine fights back and sets up the Devine-Time but Mensa reverses with a slingshot and follows up with a huge T-Bone suplex sending Devine out of the ring (on the opposite side).

Devine regains his composure and picks up the LWL belt, running at Mensa for a lethal shot (it misses) and Mensa locks in the Perfect-plex for the 1, 2 and 3.

Match Time: 12 minutes

Winner and STILL LWL Champion: Mat Mensa (c)

Another good match on a good card of wrestling action, Devine and Mensa produced a back and forth match that could have gone either way. In a match where it looked like only an error would end it, Devine's attempt at cheating backfired on him and Mensa retained the LWL title. Great way to end a good show from LWL!

First off congratulations to LWL on increasing their attendance even after the ring broke last time! The fans that turned up were introduced to a good wrestling show from top to bottom, first time seeing Sykes and boy did that guy impress, a truly sensational performance by him. Navarro looked very good also and if a rematch is booked between the two, it will be worth the £5 entrance fee alone.

Ryder and Costello brought the comedy to the show, Maxx vs Dutt, and Devine vs Mensa brought two competitive and good matches in their own right to a very good card produced by LWL. This card like many of the other British Wrestling cards I have been too deserved to be seen by more than 52 people!

Match of the Night:
Sykes vs Kris Navarro

A Road Trip to Wales

Even though I had 1PW 2nd Year Anniversary (the next day) when Mad Dog Maxx offered me the opportunity to watch him vs Tracy Smothers at Celtic Wrestling 'Big Bang 3' in Cardiff, Wales I jumped at the chance. I also really wanted to meet interviewee Justin Johnson who was wrestling on the show.

It was cool talking to Maxx about the business especially our lengthy chat on World Championship Wrestling. We got lost once in Wales and ironically Justin was sent out to meet us. My memory is a little hazy about the show, I remember enjoying the show, especially Maxx vs Smothers and meeting Matt Vaughn, Caiman, Tracy Smothers and of course Justin Johnson. We got back in the early hours and Russ dropped me home.

1PW 2nd Year Anniversary (13th October 2007)

Once again, I have misplaced my full 1PW 2nd Year Anniversary report, below are just the best bits.

Martin Stone vs Scorpio

Crowd are appreciative of both men with "Welcome back" chants and "Let's go Scorpio/Let's go Stone" duelling chants before the match starts. Stone gains advantage of the first lock-up, backing Scorpio into the corner. Slapping Scorpio's chest before breaking. On the second lock-up Scorpio reverses and Stone goes into the corner, Stone pushes Scorpio down and Scorpio shows Stone the finger. This was a pretty even match with neither man gaining a clear cut advantage as the match progressed.

Scorpio and Stone are pretty evenly matched with no one winning the test of strength battle, Scorpio hits Stone with a top rope leg-drop, Stone wisely rolls onto his front, Scorpio can only get a two count. Scorpio motions for the 450 but is caught in a roll up pin by Stone for a two count.

"Let's go Martin/Let's go Scorpio!" chants once more as the fans can't decide who they like best. Stone hits Scorpio with a German suplex for another two count, Scorpio fires back with a punch and a roundhouse kick downing Stone.

Scorpio motions for the 450 once more but instead hits Stone with a moonsault leg drop for the 1, 2 and 3. The fans clap as both men shake hands, chanting, "1PW!" and, "Please come back!" as both men bow to each other.

Match Time: 19 minutes

Winner: Scorpio

That was a very good match, evenly contested from the start. Good wrestling from both men and the fans cheering for both added to the atmosphere, either man could have won that match and if a rematch happens at some point down the road, I welcome it.

45 Minute Iron Man Match for 1PW Openweight Title

Darren Burridge vs Nigel McGuinness (c)

The fans once again have no clear favourite as they chant, "Let's go Darren/Let's go Nigel!" The competitors lock-up Burridge pushes McGuinness into the ropes and breaks cleanly. McGuinness comes back with an armlock but Burridge quickly gets to the ropes, McGuinness breaks cleanly also. McGuinness locks Burridge in a footlock, Burridge reverses out into a waistlock takedown, the fans chant "Woo, woo!" in support of Burridge.

Burridge turns the waistlock into an armlock but McGuinness rolls out into a waistlock of his own, transferring into a full nelson, Burridge rolls McGuinness up for a two count. "Let's go Nigel/Let's go Darren" duelling chants once more, McGuinness has Burridge in a leg scissors, cleverly Burridge rolls himself into a medicine ball and escapes! European uppercuts are traded and then a series of pinfalls which McGuinness gets the best of for the 1, 2 and 3.

1st Fall Time: 11 minutes

Winner: Nigel McGuinness

McGuinness 1 Burridge 0

The competitors shake hands to chants of "Nigel/Darren." A test of strength follows Burridge rolls out, trips McGuinness and applies the armlock once more, McGuinness rolls through and escapes. "Let's go Nigel/Let's go Darren" chants once more, Burridge locks McGuinness in the Haas of Pain but McGuinness manages to get to the ropes.

Once again Burridge breaks cleanly, Burridge and McGuinness then do a series of old school British wrestling manoeuvres with Burridge getting the better of McGuinness and a quick pinfall equals the match up.

2nd Fall Time: 7 minutes

Winner: Darren Burridge

McGuinness 1 Burridge 1

McGuinness throws an elbow at Burridge, and then throws Burridge out of the ring. McGuinness rams Burridge's head off the guardrail and then rolls in and out (breaking up the Referee's count), McGuinness runs at Burridge and with a lariat knocks Burridge and the guardrail up in the air! "Nigel/Darren" duelling chants once more, back in the ring McGuinness gets caught by a discus lariat of Burridge for a two count.

McGuinness tries for a suplex but Burridge blocks, causing McGuinness to once again elbow Burridge in the head. McGuinness attempts the Tower of London but misses, Burridge seizes the opportunity but gets crotched on the turnbuckle, this time McGuinness hits the Tower of London for the 1, 2 and 3.

3rd Fall Time: 5 minutes

Winner: Nigel McGuinness

McGuinness 2 Burridge 1

McGuinness throws Burridge head first into the turnbuckle, and quickly follows up with a two count. Burridge comes back with a roll up of his own for a two count also. McGuinness hits a trip and elbow to Burridge for another two count. "Let's go Nigel/Let's go Darren" chants once again.

Burridge hits an uppercut on McGuinness who responds with a club to the back and uses up the Referee's 5 count. Burridge zeroes in on McGuinness's arm and with the Rings of Saturn locked in McGuinness taps out. The fans finally decide to lend their support to Darren Burridge in this contest.

4th Fall Time: 6 minutes

Winner: Darren Burridge

McGuinness 2 Burridge 2

Burridge and McGuinness take it to the outside, Burridge slams McGuinness's arm on the guardrail, following up with an armbreaker on the apron. Burridge applies the Fujiwara armbar, shaking the arm as the fans chant, "Easy!" Burridge traps McGuinness's arm but McGuinness rolls him up for a two count.

Backslide by Burridge for a two count, McGuinness rolls Burridge up even grabbing the tights but can only manages a two count. "Let's go Nigel/Let's go Darren" chants from the 1PW fans, both men trade slaps and then Burridge hits a lariat of his own for the 1, 2 and 3.

5th Fall Time: 8 minutes

Winner: Darren Burridge

McGuinness 2 Burridge 3

McGuinness hangs Burridge on the top rope, following up with an uppercut and a back elbow before both men exchange chops. A suplex follows by Burridge for a two count, Burridge once again locks in the Rings of Saturn but McGuinness reaches the ropes, so Burridge pulls him back to the centre of the ring and applies it again.

"Let's go Nigel/Let's go Darren" chants once more, Burridge stretches McGuinness like a pretzel. Fans chant "Woo, Woo!" in support of Burridge once more. McGuinness returns with a chinbreaker and crotches Burridge on the ropes, McGuinness misses the follow up lariat but nails Burridge with a lariat to the back of the head for the 1, 2 and 3.

6th Fall Time: 6 minutes

Winner: Nigel McGuinness

McGuinness 3 Burridge 3

McGuinness doesn't have much time to celebrate as Burridge quickly applies the small package and gets a 3 count of his own!

7th Fall Time: 1 minute

Winner: Darren Burridge

McGuinness 3 Burridge 4

With a minute left in the match, Burridge decides running is the best course of action, McGuinness follows and connects with a lariat for a two count only. McGuinness quickly follows up with a short arm lariat but can only get a two count once more! Both men trade slaps and McGuinness connects with a vicious third lariat and gains 1, 2 and 3 with just seconds remaining!

"That was awesome!" chants from the 1PW crowd as they clap both men, "That was Wrestling," chant starts up, and as both men shake hands and hug, the fans chant, "One more time."

8th Fall Time: 1 minute

Winner: Nigel McGuinness

McGuinness 4 Burridge 4

Match Time: 45 minutes

Winner: Draw - Nigel McGuinness retains 1PW Openweight Title (c)

WOW! That was a fantastic match and well worth the £10-£65 admission fee alone, both men brought their 'A' game to the Doncaster Dome tonight and produced a match of the year candidate that left the 1PW fans in awe. I loved how the story progressed in the match, a matter of respect in the first couple of falls, McGuinness then using legal but cowardly tactics in the next few falls and finally the desperation in the last minute to equal the match. The fans really came alive in this match with constant chants for both competitors for the entire 45 minutes. I echo the fans who chanted "One more time" as I could probably watch Burridge and McGuinness wrestle all day!

Tag Team Lumberjack Match for 1PW Tag Titles
Damned Nation (Dragon Aisu & Majik w/Gabriel Grey and 5 lumberjacks) vs The Dragonhearts (Spud & Luke 'Dragon' Phoenix w/Dean Ayass and 5 lumberjacks) (c)

A video shows highlighting The Dragonhearts vs Damned Nation feud. Britrage (Mark Sloan & Wade Fitzgerald) watch on from the entrance ramp.

The Dragonhearts have a disagreement with some of the 1PW fans at ringside. Phoenix and Majik start the match to, "Let's go Phoenix/Let's go Majik" duelling chants. Majik hooks Phoenix in a waistlock and brings him to the mat, they tie-up again and this time Phoenix brings Majik to the mat and adds a few slaps to head just for good measure. Another waistlock attempt follows, it's reversed out of and into a two count by Phoenix, Majik recovers and applies the abdominal stretch but Phoenix once again turns it into a pinfall for a two count.

Majik counters with a cradle of his own for a two count, Phoenix hits Majik with a snapmere into a pin for another two count. The fans are split on the two teams with "Damned Nation/Suck" duelling chants, Aisu applies the figure four on Phoenix as the fans chant "1PW" Phoenix's shoulders hit the mat and the Referee reaches a two count. Phoenix manages to reverse the pressure, Spud pulls the rope back. Majik enters and kicks Phoenix in the head, Spud chases after Majik and is pulled to outside, cue an all-out war between the lumberjacks!

Ring Announcer Stevie Aaron makes his way into the ring, removing his shirt to reveal a Damned Nation T-Shirt! Superkick by Stevie to Aisu!! He takes off Damned Nation shirt to reveal a 1PW one. Spud follows up with a splash but it is only a nearfall, Grey enters with a cane, Ayass cuts him off and then hits Spud!

Ayass takes jacket off to reveal a Damned Nation T-Shirt, Ayass follows up with a cane shot to Phoenix's injured knee, Majik pins Spud 1, 2, no! Spud gets his shoulder up. Damned Nation berate the Ref as they are in disbelief, fans chant "1PW" once again. Aisu and Majik hit the elevated Flatliner for the 1, 2 and 3.

"There are champions," "Thank you, Ayass," "Twisted Genius," "Damned Nation/Suck" duelling chant, "You're our Champions," "We want tears," directed at Spud and finally, "1PW" chant during the aftermath of the match.

Match Time: 31 minutes

Winners and NEW 1PW Tag Team Champions: Damned Nation (Dragon Aisu & Majik w/Gabriel Grey) (c)

That was a fantastic match! A great advertisement for tag team wrestling, the lumberjacks added a lot to the match as the fans went crazy when they fought each other as it felt like an all-out war. The atmosphere was the greatest I have heard in the two year history of 1PW, it was absolutely electric. The fans were divided between the Dragonhearts and the Damned Nation, and became pretty pro-Damned Nation during the match.

Everyone believed Aaron was the mole, so his superkick to Aisu was a huge surprise as was Ayass turning his back on Spud! The nearfalls that followed created an edge of your seat ending to the match, Damned Nation vs The Dragonhearts or even Damned Nation vs Britrage would be two matches I would like to see in the future.

Stone vs Scorpio was a good technical wrestling match, the 45 minute Iron Man was absolutely superb and a must see when the show comes out on DVD! Damned Nation vs The Dragonhearts not only produced a very good match but the greatest atmosphere in 1PW history.

Slam Wrestling

Date: Friday 19th October 2007
Time: 7:00pm
Attendance: 171
Price: £5 Child, £10 Adult
Location: Tamworth Assembly Halls, Tamworth, West Midlands.

Hollie is your Ring Announcer for the evening.

The Headmaster vs Chip Durant

Headmaster's weight advantage allows him to control the early going, by easily pushing Durant off. Even with the weight advantage Headmaster still feels the need to cheat (by raking Durant's face across the ropes), only breaking just before the 5 count. Headmaster looks to have the match won, but instead of taking the pin he pulls Durant up before the 3 count!

The fans chant, "You suck!" at Headmaster, Headmaster goes for a top rope splash but misses allowing Durant to hit the leg lariat for the 1, 2 and 3. Durant adds insult to injury (slapping Headmaster's head as he leaves). Hilarious moment as the Ring Announcer forgets who won "Winner of the match Headmaster erm… Chip Durant."

Match Time: 7 minutes

Winner: Chip Durant

A few errors stopped this match from being anything more than decent, but to be fair to the two competitors they managed to keep the match together and it ended up being a decent contest.

Cypher vs Yel Darb 'The Viking'

Cyber attacks Darb from behind, a Polish hammer by Darb ends that. Darb then smacks Cypher's head on each level of the turnbuckle, and follows up with a clothesline which downs Cypher (who leaves the ring shortly after). Darb follows and rolls him back in and with a club to the back, this match is over!

Match Time: 2 minutes

Winner: Yel Darb 'The Viking'

That was quick! A blink and you just may miss it match, Darb's power advantage was just too much for Cypher, producing an okay match for the time given.

Killer Instinct (Tiger X & Angelblade) vs Jexodus (Jekkel & Exodus)

Killer Instinct attack from behind, but Jexodus fight back with double dropkicks and a bear hug/splash combination. Exodus continues the attack with a big boot on Tiger, and a hiptoss into a neckbreaker on Angelblade. Quick tags are traded between Jexodus as they cut the ring in half, keeping Tiger in their corner. Killer Instinct fight back and take control of the match successfully keeping Exodus isolated from his partner Jekkel, that is until there is a double tag made (which makes the fans go crazy)!

Jekkel takes Killer Instinct down with clotheslines and powerslams, following up with a Jekkel driver which is broken up, leading to a double chokeslam on Blade. Jexodus set Tiger up for a doomsday device, Blade low blows Exodus and Tiger reverses into a victory roll for the 1, 2 and 3.

Match Time: 10 minutes

Winners: Killer Instinct (Tiger X & Angelblade)

That was a good old school tag match, both teams produced and the fans loved every second of it. With the way the match ended it looks like a rematch could be on the cards and I'm all for that.

'Playboy' Phil Bedwell vs 'Wonderkid' Jonny Storm

Bedwell takes the microphone. "Shut your mouths and open your eyes, or are you stupid as well as ugly?" Bedwell continues, "I'm a real man here to make your dull little lives interesting, for the wives, the mothers and all the lovers it's ALL about the love." Bedwell leaves as Storm enters, even stealing a kid's shoe. Gyrations by Bedwell (the fans boo), gyrations by Storm (fans cheer), posing came next with the same response.

Bedwell frustrated pushes Storm down, Storm comes right back and pushes Bedwell down. Hiptoss reversals follow until Storm hiptosses Bedwell out of the ring to the floor below. Bedwell begs off and then throws Storm into the buckle, he misses with the follow up allowing Storm to catch him in an armlock, Bedwell is able to reverse out, but Storm reverses once more skilfully using the ropes to apply an armbar. Bedwell sets up for a Pedigree but gets caught in the Wonderwhirl only to reverse into another Pedigree but that only manages to get a two count.

The fans chant, "Jonny, Jonny!" and "Loser, Loser!" at Bedwell, a backdrop by Storm sets Bedwell up for the 6-1-9 which he delivers, Storm follows up with a moonsault for a two count. Bedwell returns with a low-blow (in front of the Referee) which strangely doesn't end the match with a DQ! Bedwell pushes Storm into a corner but Storm comes back with a step up Enzuguri for the 1, 2 and 3. The fans clap and stamp their feet for Storm.

Match Time: 14 minutes

Winner: 'Wonderkid' Jonny Storm

That was a good match, the best match of the night thus far. Storm and Bedwell performed well and the fans seemed to enjoy it. Not sure why the Ref didn't DQ Bedwell for the illegal low-blow, right in front of him. Finish out of nowhere, so I'm hoping to see a rematch between the two down the line.

INTERMISSION

Jetta vs Stephanie Scope

Jetta gargles on Water, the fans chant, "Time-Waster!" at her. A young kid stamps on Jetta's toes, so she takes the microphone. "Well you've done a good job raising him, a young man attacking a woman!" Jetta continues, "Can you keep the noise down, I can't concentrate." Jetta and Scope pose on the turnbuckles with Jetta being booed while Scope is cheered. Jetta takes a few moments to pull up knee pads, when questioned she replies, "Safety first."

Scope's power is too much for Jetta and after being pushed off during a lock-up she leaves. Jetta returns for another lock-up and once again is pushed down, Jetta pulls Scope's hair and then attacks her from behind. A fan shouts, "Jetta's ugly" to which she replies, "So is your mom!" Fans clap for Scope, Jetta tells them "No, no, no, Shhhhhhhhh."

Scope returns with a sideslam for a two count. Scope misses the follow up and goes head first into the buckle, Jetta hits a clothesline and applies the armbar, another clothesline follows shortly after.

Scope ducks a third and applies the backslide for a two count, a schoolgirl follows for another two, Jetta tackles Scope and with her feet on the ropes gets the 1, 2 and 3.

Match Time: 10 minutes

Winner: Jetta

That was a good woman's contest, with both women performing well in front of the Slam fans. Jetta showed why she is becoming a worldwide talent (after a recent trip to Shimmer in the U.S.A.) and Scope showed why she may join her one day. With the ending, a rematch may happen in the future and I for one would like to see that.

Prince Osmond w/Tenacious D vs Shabazz

Tenacious D takes the microphone. "You are ugly losers, but even I didn't expect it to be as a bad as this!"

Osmond takes the microphone. "Do you know who I am, do you know who my father is!?" the fans chant, "Who are ya?"

Tenacious D takes the microphone again. "I'm Tenacious by name and nature, Shabazz isn't good enough to lick Osmond's boot." The two competitors lock-up and Osmond pushes Shabazz off, in the corner he pushes Shabazz's chest and breaks.

Shabazz fires back with a slap, follow up clotheslines don't move Osmond but a leg lariat does (the crowd goes crazy!). "Fight!" chant starts up, as Osmond leaves the ring, followed shortly after by

Shabazz. Osmond hits a running powerslam but only gets a two count, he then boots Shabazz out of the ring, Tenacious D continues the assault. Shabazz manages to reverse an Irish whip and quickly hits an RKO, Tenacious D distracts the Referee as the fans chant, "One more time!" Tenacious D holds onto Shabazz's leg and Osmond follows up with a DVD for the 1, 2 and 3.

Match Time: 8 minutes

Winner: Prince Osmond w/Tenacious D

Decent match between the two competitors, Osmond looks like he is new to Professional Wrestling, he's not a bad wrestler but there is room for improvement. Shabazz looked competitive in losing and a rematch should be on the cards based on the way the match ended.

Handicap Match

Stixx & The Murderers vs Paul Malen

Stixx takes the microphone. "Shut up! I felt it in my stomach and throat, the smell of you fans makes me want to throw up!" Stixx continues, "My student (Paul Malen) turned his back on me because he cared more about what you fans thought! That makes me a very angry man."

Malen rushes in and gets a 3 on 1 beat down, double clothesline and dropkicks by Malen downs The Murderers whilst Stixx runs away. Malen reverses an Irish whip and hits hiptosses on all three men, Malen continues the attack with forearms and a monkey flip until he is attacked by a Murderer. Malen hits a reverse DDT and DDT combination on The Murderers, Jonny Storm joins him to chants of, "Jonny," Malen finally makes the tag and Storm hits a double clothesline on The Murderers and a flying head scissors on Stixx.

Double noggin-knocker follows and a double 6-1-9. Storm low bridges Stixx (sending him to the outside), followed by a slingshot cross body, Malen hits a Murderer with a Flatliner for the 1, 2 and 3. "You suck and loser" chants follow for Stixx and his team as Storm and Malen celebrate.

Match Time: 13 minutes

Winners: Paul Malen & 'Wonderkid' Jonny Storm

That was good main event to finish the show with. I was surprised by the handicap match stipulation and I was shocked by Jonny Storm's entrance into the match! As far as handicap matches go, it was one of the better ones I have seen.

A solid show, a few errors in the first match took away from it. Yarb squashed Cypher, the tag match was good for the time allotted, Storm vs Bedwell was good as well and match of the night. The women's match was good, Osmond vs Shabazz was an ok match and the handicapped match was a good way to end the show.

I think £10 for an adult for a solid show is a bit too much for the fans to pay and should probably be looked at. 171 for an audience on a Friday night is impressive though!

Match of the Night:
'Playboy' Phil Bedwell vs 'Wonderkid' Jonny Storm

AWW

Date: Thursday 25th October 2007
Time: 8:00pm
Attendance: 123
Price: £5
Location: Irish Centre, Digbeth, Birmingham, West Midlands.

Stu Smith is your Ring Announcer for the evening.

Tommy Gunn vs 'Desirable' Danny D

Danny still wears the dress he was forced to wear months earlier and there are "Tommy Gunn" chants for Gunn. Lock-up, Danny pushes Gunn off. "I don't hit Girls," Gunn retorts, Danny replies with punches that floor Gunn. Danny whips Gunn into the ropes, Gunn ducks the clothesline and returns with a hurricanrana and a head scissors in quick succession. Gunn then low bridges Danny to chants of, "Easy!" from the AWW fans.

The fans continue to rally behind Gunn with chants of "Tommy, Tommy," Gunn responds with punches and a leg lariat to Danny's face. A clothesline, drop toe hold and 6-1-9 follow and with a springboard splash Gunn has it won! No it's only a two count, Danny returns with a vicious clothesline that flips Gunn in the air and sets up for a tombstone piledriver but somehow Gunn reverses into a pin for the 1, 2 and 3.

Match Time: 10 minutes

Winner: Tommy Gunn

Good opening match which the AWW fans seemed to enjoy! Gunn and Danny put forth a good display and it transferred into a good match. Gunn has a lot of potential as both a singles wrestler and tag team wrestler (with Geraden as The Young Gunns). Danny is a good wrestler in his own right and the character works well. I was disappointed that Geraden was missing from the show after The Young Gunns strong showing against Ronin and Derice Coffie last month.

8 Man Battle Royal (For the Last Spot in Rumble at Aston University)

'Star Man' Mark Clarke vs Matt Clarke vs Jekkel vs El Nacho vs Lord Graham Thomas vs Lee Hunter vs Derice Coffie vs Nick Knight

This match was fast and furious with action all over the ring! Matt Clarke tries but fails to eliminate Knight, Coffie hits a vicious high knee in the corner and then is gorilla pressed and thrown out of the ring by Jekkel!

Derice Coffie has been eliminated.

Jekkel tries to eliminate both Clarke's but they low bridge him and he too is eliminated.

Jekkel has been eliminated.

LGT quickly eliminates El Nacho

Knight eliminates Matt Clarke, LGT follows shortly after.

Knight is alone with Mark Clarke & Lee Hunter. Knight shows his power advantage by gorilla pressing and the slamming on Clarke, a face wash follows (on both men). Before Knight summoning his Cruiserweight power hits two awe inspiring tumbling splashes on Clarke & Hunter! Knight calls for a powerbomb but only receives a step up Enzuguri from Hunter, two double dropkicks follow on Knight and he too is eliminated.

Nick Knight has been eliminated.

Hunter pie faces Clarke leading to both men trading punches, Hunter atomic drops Clarke almost over the top rope. Clarke returns with a leg lariat and a powerslam on Clarke, before throwing Hunter but not eliminating him. Hunter replies with a leg lariat of his own and tries to eliminate Clarke. Clarke summons strength and back body drops Hunter over the top rope to win the Battle Royal.

Lee Hunter has been eliminated.

Match Time: 9 minutes

Winner: 'Star Man' Mark Clarke

Well that was chaotic! With so much action going on it was very difficult to keep up with it all, most of the eliminations were blink and you might miss it. All the competitors put forth a good performance especially Nick Knight. Clarke and Hunter showed intensity that I haven't seen before in the finale between the two.

With the match going 9 minutes (for 8 men) it was never going to be a classic, with more time a better match could have happened for sure, with that said this was fun and a different element to the show.

'The Metro-Sexual' Danny Devine vs British Born Steele

Devine attacks BBS before the bell even sounds, BBS rallies and hits a few chops as the fans chant, "B-B-S." Devine backs off and even pleads with BBS for a sportsman like handshake, BBS asks the crowd and then shakes Devine's hand. Devine tries to gain an advantage but BBS catches his boot and swings to the Ref before kicking Devine's leg and taking him down to the mat. Devine locks in the Boston Crab but BBS manages to get the escape via a rope break.

Devine comes back with a sunset flip for a two count, BBS returns with his finishing move (The Backcracker) but doesn't have enough left to cover Devine and when he does it's only a close nearfall. BBS shows frustration by pulling Devine's hair and sets up for a victory roll but Devine reverses and with his feet on the ropes takes the 1, 2 and 3.

Match Time: 10 minutes

Winner: 'The Metro-Sexual' Danny Devine

Aftermath:
BBS takes the microphone and asks the Referee, "What the bloody hell was that?" before pushing him down! He continues, "It's been 8 months since I last won a match here." The fans show their disdain with

"Who are ya?" chants, BBS retorts with, "Shut your mouth, son." BBS continues, "I was the first ever AWW Champion, you should respect me! You fans haven't helped me regain MY title so I'll get it myself!"

This was a really good match, with great storytelling (BBS's growing frustration, Devine's cheating and then BBS turning his back on the fans). It will be interesting to see where BBS goes from here, and that is something I will be watching intently.

Chained Match (First To Touch All 4 Corners, Wins the Match)

Mad Dog Maxx vs Dan Ryder

Maxx tells the fans, "Ryder's going down, scumbags!"

The fans chant, "Mad Dog has rabies!"

Maxx retorts, "Mad Dog doesn't have rabies, swig your point and watch wrestling!"

The fans start chanting, "Ryder, Ryder!"

There is a feeling out period to start the match with neither man wanting to make a mistake. Punches are traded with Ryder getting the best of it, ramming Maxx head first into the steel ringpost. Ryder follows up with a clothesline and a hurricanrana before he touches 3 out of the 4 Corners, Maxx cuts him off with a chain assisted throat chop.

Ryder blocks a clothesline and returns with a couple of his own, following up with a 10 punch in the corner and a monkey flip. Ryder follows with a back body drop but misses the resulting 450, both men are down Mad Dog has something in his hand!

FIREBALL to Ryder!! Maxx then touches all 4 corners for the win. Maxx then continues the assault and drags Ryder by the chain away.

Match Time: 12 minutes

Winner: Mad Dog Maxx

That was a very good match, the best of the night thus far! It was intense, had comedy-esque moments, good wrestling and a truly WOW finish to the match. The fans are a little fickle in AWW, when I saw Ryder in April he was the biggest star in the company. The fans went crazy for him, now he's competing for cheers with Maxx and at times is losing out.

I'm slightly fearful for Ryder as the fans seem to be slowly turning their back on him. Maxx was exceptional once more proving that he is a very good wrestler with a great character (The fans seem to love him for the latter). The finish came out of nowhere and brings an even higher level of intensity to the most intense feud of 2007 in AWW.

INTERMISSION

Ronin vs Carnage

The wrestlers lock-up, with Ronin getting the best of it (pushing Carnage down). Second time around neither man budges so they say, "Sumo!" and in sumo stance try to knock each other down. A test of strength proceeds which Ronin gets the advantage of and with a kick downs Carnage. Carnage rolls out to strategize, and comes back with kicks to Ronin's leg trying to knot it up.

Ronin attempts the 10 punch in the corner but Carnage powerbombs him to the mat! Carnage quickly follows up with a leg drop and top rope elbow drop but can only get a two count. Spud enters and spits at Carnage, Ronin hits Carnage with his Singapore Cane and with a big splash it's over 1, 2, and 3.

Match Time: 9 minutes

Winner: Ronin

That wasn't a very good match, both styles clashed and in the end I was glad the match was over. Ronin's more of a Character than a Wrestler so it's understandable that his wrestling skills aren't as good as say a Danny Devine or BBS.

Carnage is use to wrestling good 'pure' wrestlers and this wasn't the case tonight. On the plus side the ending to the match has advanced the Spud vs Carnage storyline and that is good for AWW.

'Human Hate Machine' Moralez vs Marcus Kool

Moralez shows complete disrespect for Kool by slapping him across the face, it turned out to be mistake as it just fired up Kool! Who returned with a slap and punch of his own, a clothesline and dropkick followed in quick succession. Kool drop toe holds Moralez but when attempting the 6-1-9, Moralez rolls to the outside. Kool not perturbed quickly follows with a slingshot splash over the ropes, then the two competitors take the match around the Irish Centre. Kool calls for, "Sweet chin music, baby!"

Moralez blocks but Kool reverses into a side effect for a close nearfall. Kool goes up top but misses with a Swanton Bomb, Moralez makes Kool pay with a vicious club and sit-down powerbomb but Kool kicks out! Moralez sets up another powerbomb but Kool reverses Moralez onto the middle rope, and quickly follows with a 6-1-9 but that only gets a 2 count (Kool can't believe it!) Moralez goes for Kool but he ducks, Moralez viciously clubs him to the back and gets the 1, 2 and 3. The fans show their appreciation to Kool with loud clapping as he leaves the ring.

Match Time: 12 minutes

Winner: 'Human Hate Machine' Moralez

That was a superb match! I wasn't sure what match of the night would be but it's going to be incredibly hard to top this match. Kool and Moralez brought their 'A' game to the Irish Centre on this night and produced a breathless match for the fans in attendance. The nearfalls towards the end of this match made the fans gasp, and move to the edge of seats.

Moralez showed why he is one of the best big men in the UK and Kool shows why he has potential to become one of the best in the UK also. That was a match that made me proud to report on Professional Wrestling, and I would love to see a rematch at some point down the road.

'Rockstar' Spud vs 'Wonderkid' Jonny Storm

Storm takes the microphone. "It's good to be back in AWW!"

"Super Gran," chant starts up after a lady attacks Spud. Storm and Spud contest a hiptoss, reversing until Spud goes over the top rope to the floor below. Spud runs away from Storm, Storm catches up with him and after an armdrag applies the armlock, paint brushing Spud's head as he does, hilariously Spud tells the Referee, "It hurts!"

An airplane spin knocks the Ref down, Spud hits a jumping DDT but when he covers the Ref is down, he blows snot on Storm! Storm replies with a Wonderwhirl but once again the Ref is still down. Spud low blows Storm and hits with a Stunner, Carnage enters allowing Storm to roll Spud up for the 1, 2 and 3. Spud chokes the Ref and then hilariously trips himself up as he leaves the ring.

Match Time: 13 minutes

Winner: 'Wonderkid' Jonny Storm

Another electric atmosphere created by the AWW fans, the duelling chants and entire noise made it difficult for me to think! Spud and Storm took part in a fine contest and a good way to finish the wrestling action for the night.

Spud's Rockstar character is like a breath of fresh air and Storm was just his usual entertaining self. Once again the Spud vs Carnage storyline has been progressed, so this match had good wrestling and booking which is just what the fans want from Pro Wrestling show.

Dan Ryder's Announcement:
Ryder comes out with a bandage over his eye and takes the microphone. "I've never had my face burnt! I have been given opportunity to pick the match of choice, Hardcore (nope), TLC (loud cheer) not that either, at Aston University Me vs Mad Dog Maxx in a Steel Cage!"

The fans love that. Maxx interrupts and with a lariat levels Ryder! Maxx shouts, "Dan Ryder you have just signed your death warrant."

That was an effective segment, Ryder showed no fear by challenging Maxx to a Cage Match. Maxx's beat down was pretty brutal including the lariat that flipped Ryder. Ryder is a crazy S.O.B. in the ring and I can't even imagine what he will do in his quest to beat Maxx in the Cage Match (30th November 2007). In a match I will be watching with baited breath.

Tommy Gunn has a lot of potential and Danny D's entertaining as hell creating a good match between to two. I hope to see the Young Gunn's (Geraden/Gunn) tagging once more soon though! The Battle Royal was rushed but produced some WOW moments like Knight's tumbling splash. BBS vs Devine wasn't as good as last month's perfect match, but it was good in its own merit and I wonder where BBS will go (after he turned his back on fans).

Ryder vs Maxx was intense and had a WOW finish to end the match, Moralez vs Kool was a superb match with incredible nearfalls. Spud vs Storm was a good match with an electric atmosphere, to end the wrestling on the show. Maxx vs Ryder in a

Cage should be a treat come (30th November), another very good show put forth by AWW. They also deserve to be congratulated for the increase in attendance from 72 (last month) to 123 this month!

Match of the Night:
'Human Hate Machine' Moralez vs Marcus Kool

A Trip to Luton

I met up with Danny Devine, Dan Ryder, Miss Ryder and Geraden and we travelled down to Luton for Power Trip Wrestling's 'Hardcore Halloween.' No issues this time round we got there and they prepared while I watched the show.

The possibility of Sykes vs The Legendary Johnny Kidd was salivating – I still cannot believe this match didn't happen!

The guys as 3-Some a Money Making Team (that no one capitalized on) & Geraden had a good match - I was really impressed with his partner Ghetto G. It was good catching up with TBW Champion Shabazz but The highlight was meeting and shaking hands with Johnny Kidd.

Legends Wrestling League

Date: Tuesday 30th October 2007
Time: 7:30pm
Attendance: 162
Price: Adults £5, £4 with LWL Flyer (Downloadable from http://www.lwluk.co.uk) Kids £3. £1 off if you wear Fancy dress to this show.

Location: Legends Members Club, Oxley Street, Wolverhampton, West Midlands, WV1 1QN.

The Ring Announcer welcomes the crowd to LWL's 2nd Anniversary and comments on how there is only standing room inside the Legend's Members Club this evening.

Platinum Page vs Kris Navarro

The contest starts with an armdrag by Navarro, followed quickly by a couple of hip-tosses and an Enzuguri. The fans clap, Page cuts Navarro off with a short elbow, and chokes him with his boot. Kicks to the back and chops to front and back follow as he starts to control the match, a snap suplex gets the first pinfall attempt of the night (for a two count). Page knees Navarro in the back and applies a chinlock. "You're not cheering for him now!" The fans start clapping and slamming against the tables. Page locks Navarro in a mid-ring sleeper hold, after Navarro's hand drops twice he fights back.

Ducking two clothesline attempts before hitting a flying head scissors and a wheelbarrow into an armdrag. Following up with a Spear but that only manages a two count (as Page gets his foot on the ropes). A second Spear misses and Page quickly follows up with a German suplex for a close nearfall, and a huge T-Bone suplex but that gets 2 also (so he berates the Referee for the lack of 3 count). Page sets up for his Impaler finisher but Navarro rolls him up for the 1, 2 and 3.

Match Time: 9 minutes

Winner: Kris Navarro

That was a good back and forth match to start LWL's 2YA show! Navarro's performance was good once again and Page showed a good improvement over last month's slightly shaky match. I was gutted about no Sykes vs Navarro 2 after they put on a fantastic match last month, and to be honest I still am (hoping to see that feud continued at some point down the line) but this was a good way to kick off the show.

'Mr #1' Jonny Costello vs 'Sik' Nik Dutt

Costello plays limbo with the microphone cable, the match starts with a clap-off which Dutt wins. Lock-up Costello with power advantage pushes Dutt down, second time around Dutt reverses and shoulder blocks and hiptosses Costello down to the mat. Costello rolls out of the ring and rings the bell! Dutt follows with a dropkick through the ropes, Costello steals a Fans water bottle and then pulls Dutt out. Costello hits Dutt with a throat chop and another before chopping the steel ringpost!

Dutt takes control slamming Costello's hand on tables, etc. Costello kicks the rope as Dutt returns. "I'm a Champion!" Costello clotheslines Dutt right on the bridge of the nose, so Dutt in return drops him on his head with a Hurricanrana for a two count. Dutt follows up with a whip/bulldog and splash combination for another two count as Costello's foot is on the ropes. Dutt attempts the tornado DDT but Costello reverses into a full nelson slam for the 1, 2 and 3. The fans clap for Dutt as he leaves.

Match Time: 12 minutes

Winner: 'Mr #1' Jonny Costello

Another enjoyable match, good back and forth contest between the two competitors. Mistimed clothesline and hurricanrana added a lot to intensity of the match and were real OUCH moments! Costello showed he can wrestle and brawl as well as he wrestles comedy matches. Dutt put forth another good performance and that made another good match for the LWL fans to enjoy.

Mad Dog Maxx w/'Mr #1' Jonny Costello vs Tracy Smothers

Pre-Match:
Maxx endears himself to the crowd: "Shut your stinking mouths up! I'll kick your teeth down your throat!"

Smothers enters to a huge roar from the crowd, causing Maxx & Costello to roll out to the floor. Maxx is both cheered and booed as he takes the microphone. "Shut your mouth and listen to me! You may have wrestled 3 bears but tonight you're wrestling a Mad Dog. You're a rebel, a cheat and scummy. But you're a great wrestler and the king of the dance-off!"

Fans start a "Tracy Smothers, Tracy Smothers!" chant, Tracy takes the mic. "Are you all having a good time? Is it good to be alive and in Wolverhampton, Tonight?" The fans cheer loudly. "Was that the biggest piece of crap you have ever heard? You Costello are a transplant rebel and I'm going to put your head up your ass. By the time this match is done you'll have a different respect for me and all these fans."

Match:
Fans chant, "Tracy, Tracy!" once more as Maxx rolls out. "Mad Dog sucks" chant starts up. "Mad Dog doesn't suck!" he replies.

"Old poodle" is shouted out by a fan! Smothers and Maxx lock-up and after a clean break Maxx accuses Smothers of pulling his hair (which he hasn't done). Waistlocks are traded with Smothers adding a snapmere once again Maxx complains of hair pulling. The fans clap and after reversing an armlock Maxx pulls Smothers by the hair to the mat! "Cheat!" chant starts up, Wristlock once more this time Smothers gets the advantage and pulls Maxx's hair.

Maxx shouts, "Tracy's been pulling my hair, tights and poking my eyes!" and then challenges him to a dance off. The first 2 vs 1 dance-off I have seen, Maxx and Costello have some moves (but the fans still boo), Smothers is the king and wins yet another dance-off. Smothers misses a back elbow and gets caught with a vicious lariat by Maxx for a close nearfall. Smothers pokes Maxx in the eyes and hits a Flatliner for a two count. Maxx returns with a spinebuster of his own. "I swear to God it's over!" But it isn't.

Costello tries to distract Smothers but gets forearmed for his troubles, he has distracted Smothers long enough for Maxx to hit a chain assisted lariat for the 1, 2 and 3. The fans boo loudly at Maxx &

Costello and cheer loudly for Smothers with, "Tracy, Tracy!" and "Please don't go," chants.

Match Time: 23 minutes

Winner: Mad Dog Maxx

Well that was just superb! Not the most complex match but it didn't need to be. Smothers and Maxx showed just how to play with a crowd's emotions to the best effect with the match produced. The best atmosphere I have experienced since I have covered LWL shows.

Maxx and Smothers put on a good wrestling match, with great crowd interaction and a dance-off. That left a lot of fans very happy and the fans that had strangely never heard of Tracy Smothers before, now have a new hero! Great stuff all around.

INTERMISSION

Marcus Kool & LWL National Pride Champion Dan Ryder (c) vs Mr Valentino & 'The Metro-Sexual' Danny Devine

Valentino jaws with the crowd. "Old woman bow down, before me," followed by a "Let's go, Ryder!" chant.

Valentino kicks Ryder and Judo throws him to the canvas, Valentino applies the armlock, Ryder skilfully turns it into a swinging armlock and reverses out! Ryder quickly follows up with a Japanese armdrag and an armlock of his own before Valentino tags in Devine and Ryder tags in Kool. Kool hits the

6-1-9 on Devine or so he thought, Devine amazingly catches Kool and applies the Sharpshooter!

It's not locked in for long though, due to a Ryder Enzuguri, Valentino kicks Ryder's injured leg and Devine locks in the Sharpshooter on Ryder. Kool connects with a Superkick on Devine knocking him into the ropes for a 6-1-9 which Kool hits this time, Ryder struggling through the pain climbs up to the top rope and connects with a picture perfect 450 splash for the 1, 2 and 3. Kool rolls Devine out of the ring and the fans clap Ryder & Kool.

Match Time: 19 minutes

Winners: Marcus Kool & LWL National Pride Champion Dan Ryder (c)

Well that was an absolutely tremendous tag team match! From bell to bell it had everything a great tag match has, energy, isolation of one man (Ryder in this match), old school tag wrestling and a great finish (Devine's reversal of 6-1-9 into a Sharpshooter was a personal highlight!). One of the best tag matches I have seen based on action and atmosphere. Only second behind The Briscoes vs Shingo & Doi (ROH in Liverpool in March '07) as the best tag team match I've seen this year and a good contender for British Wrestling's match of the year also. The best compliment I can give this match is it's the kind of match that makes my efforts to publicize British Wrestling worthwhile!

Kristian Lees:

The fans chant "Who? and who are ya?" as Lees makes his way to the ring.

Lees asks, "Are you enjoying the show?" The fans cheer in approval "I'm not," Lees replies causing the fans to boo loudly.

"Get a haircut!" chant starts up, Lees continues, "The use of Tracy Smothers signifies to me this is a B-Show." The fans disagree. "I'm from the LWL academy like Kris Navarro (huge cheer) but I'm seen as second string!" The fans boo as Lees leaves.

Well I went from wondering who Lees was to having a good understanding of him, so I say job done. It was difficult to hear what he was saying over crowd noise though, he made the fans take notice of who he is and what he is about, now I await to see him wrestle.

TGR w/The Boss vs Chandler Scott Lee

TGR berates CSL: "You like, all of this scum (points at fans) are nothing." Slaps are traded between the two, TGR hilariously shouts, "That hurt!" punches and clotheslines by CSL follow as the fans chant, "Only one Paul Bearer," at The Boss. CSL feigns hitting TGR and instead connects with a dropkick, TGR chokes CSL in the ropes and The Boss chokes him further with his tie. A nonchalant cover by TGR isn't enough to put CSL away though.

CSL whips TGR into the corner and goes for the 10 punch but TGR reverses into a running powerbomb but only manages to get a two count! So he berates the Referee, CSL hits a bulldog on TGR and goes to attack The Boss (he ducks down) and connects with his organizer to CSL's head and with a

Flatliner this match is over, 1, 2 and 3 count follows. The fans boo TGR as he leaves.

Match Time: 11 minutes

Winner: TGR w/The Boss

Not a bad match by any means. TGR and CSL put forth a solid wrestling performance, the fan interaction was there also but this was at the point where a normal LWL show would be coming to a close, so that took a little away from the match. Solid match though, so definitely not a downer on a great show thus far!

Darkstar vs Donny Bull

Darkstar spits in Bull's face (not a smart idea!), Bull takes revenge by showing that Darkstar isn't tall enough for a test of strength with him. Bull continues with chops causing Darkstar to hilariously scream, "Arrggghhh!" and "Oh my god!" The fans clap as Bull slingshot senton's over the top rope! A Bull-Hole Slam follows and finally a big splash for the 1, 2 and 3. Darkstar falls down between the ring and stage!

Match Time: 3 minutes

Winner: Donny Bull

Well that was short, sweet and to the point! Darkstar's hilarious shouting added a lot to this match, Bull has potential and is incredibly agile (slingshot senton) for a big man. So this match got across Bull as new monster of LWL (if that is the case), so from that perspective not a bad match to have just before the main event.

Hardcore Rules Wolverhampton Street Fight for LWL Championship

Sykes vs Mat Mensa (c)

Official ring introductions for both men, "Wearing a Mensa shirt eh, Grandad?" says Sykes to a fan in the crowd.

"Let's go Mensa!" chant starts up.

"This isn't a popularity contest," retorts Sykes who then wipes himself all over with towel and throws it into Mensa's face. A fan shouts obscenities at Sykes, so Sykes confronts him, the fans show their support for Sykes (in this instance). The fans then rally back behind Mensa once more with, "Let's go, Mensa!" chants.

Sykes seamlessly turns a lock-up into a headlock from the very start. Mensa reverses out into a wristlock of his own, Sykes trips Mensa and hits an STO before tying Mensa's ankle up. Sykes climbs to the top rope and attempts a Senton but misses, Maxx appears and straight away attacks Mensa, Dutt comes out to even the odds.

Maxx & Sykes hit a 3D on Dutt. Costello interjects making it 3 on 2 until Smothers enters! Smothers helps but is shortly afterwards low bridged out of the ring. Sykes dances like Smothers (taking his eye off of Mensa) who locks in the Perfect-plex for the 1, 2 and 3.

The fans cheer Mensa, Smothers and Dutt. Mensa invites Sykes back in but with the prospect of a 3 on 1 beat down Sykes thinks better of it. Fans cheer for Mensa once again as Smothers starts up an "LWL, LWL" chant to conclude the show.

Match Time: 16 minutes

Winner and STILL LWL Champion: Mat Mensa (c)

That was a very good main event to end the show! Sykes and Mensa wrestled a good match and only used weapons infrequently during the match (including a KILLER Chair shot to Mensa by Sykes!!).

Sykes took full advantage of the NO DQ rules by cheating right in front of the Referee on numerous occasions. Mensa showed he has skills to be able to carry the LWL Title into the future. Good way to end a fantastic show!

Navarro vs Page was a good back and forth match to open the show, I still need to see Sykes vs Navarro 2 though! Dutt vs Costello was a good follow up match with two OUCH moments. Maxx vs Smothers was basic but garnered the best crowd reaction I have heard in LWL thus far, tag match was one of the most intense, energetic and enthralling I have ever seen!

Kristian Lees Promo was ok I look forward to seeing him wrestle, TGR vs CSL was a solid match in it's own right. Donny the Bull looked impressive and Darkstar was hilarious, Sykes and Mensa wrestled a very good main event with one KILLER Chair shot and a crowd pleasing ending. The Ring Announcer did a great job, and I think just under 3 hours is a good time for a show. Congratulations to LWL on improving their attendance one again from 62 (last month) to a tremendous 162 (this month).

Match of the Night:
Marcus Kool & LWL National Pride Champion Dan Ryder (c) vs Mr Valentino & ' The Metro-Sexual' Danny Devine

Sovereign World Wrestling Alliance

Date: Wednesday 31st October 2007
Time: 7:45pm
Attendance: 40
Price: £5
Location: West Bromwich Labour Club, Sandwell Rd, West Bromwich, West Midlands.

The Death-Master welcomes the crowd to SWWA.

Tucker vs TGR

Lock-up starts the contest, TGR pushes Tucker off to chants of, "TGR, TGR," the same thing happens again. This time Tucker rolls out of the ring and the chase is on, Tucker boots TGR as he re-enters the ring and exchanges chops with him before TGR hits Tucker with a sling-shot suplex. Tucker complains that TGR "is touching my ass!"

Tucker fires back with punches and suplexes TGR for a two count. TGR returns with an atomic drop/Manhattan drop combination.

Powerbomb by Tucker, Tucker distracts the referee and low-blows TGR quickly following with a

Scissors Kick. Tucker climbs to the top rope but is crotched by TGR, Tucker pushes TGR off but misses with a Frog Splash. TGR hits a couple of knees to Tucker's back and connects with The Flatliner for the 1, 2 and 3. TGR then tells Tucker, "Get out of my ring!"

Match Time: 9 minutes

Winner: TGR

That was a good back and forth match. Tucker looked impressive in both his jawing with the fans and wrestling ability, TGR performed adequately well also. Mixture of comedy and wrestling made for an enjoyable match and was the exact perfect way for SWWA to start this show.

SWWA Hall of Fame

Commissioner TGR then introduces Bodycount! The fans clap, microphone problems occur so the wrestlers decide to shout!

Bodycount is asked a series of questions:
Where are you from? Walsall.

Bodycount then talks about career ending, after a torn shoulder injury - 5 years ago.

Who is the Best SWWA Superstar? The Bouncer.

Are you returning to SWWA? Before Bodycount can answer BBS interrupts. "I have no beef with you, I'm out here to talk to you about Poison." Poison interrupts, with him and Bodycount shaking hands.

Poison says, "BBS is an opportunist and it was his Back-cracker that floored me last month."

BBS protests his innocence. "It wasn't me, it was the Bouncer!"

Poison and BBS want to fight but TGR and Bodycount break them up. TGR makes Bodycount the Special Guest Referee for BBS vs Poison later.

BBS leaves. "I'll prove you wrong!" he shouts at Poison.

That was a good segment! I went in unaware of Bodycount (I left having found out more about him), I didn't know about tension between BBS and Poison (but now I know why there is tension between them). Bodycount as Guest Referee adds an interesting dynamic to BBS vs Poison and I look forward to seeing what happens when all three men are in one ring!

Jay Icon vs Axel Adams

Icon gets the best of the lock-up and turns it into a headlock takeover and transitions into a wristlock. Test of strength is called for and once again Icon drops Adams, the fans chant, "Axel, Axel!" Axel reverses out of a headlock to get to the ropes. Icon hilariously claims Adams was pulling his hair (when he is bald!).

Axel attempts a clothesline but it is reversed into a high knee by Icon, who quickly follows up with a spinning heel kick for a two count. "Long haired freak" shouts Icon, TGR makes his way to the ring and in the process distracts Icon who is rolled up by Adams for the 1, 2 and 3. TGR and Icon square off after the match.

Match Time: 26 minutes

Winner: Axel Adams

That was a good match. Adams and Icon worked well against each other and it produced a good match for the SWWA fans. Once again like the opening match it had a mixture of comedy and wrestling and that worked effectively.

The match though went too long though (26 minutes for a mid card match is too much), this match would have been better had it shaved 10-11 minutes off so it was down to 15 minutes.

The Emotional Express (Tommy White & Steve Valentino) vs The Clarke Foundation (Matt/Mark Clarke)

T.C.F. start the match fast by giving T.E.E. a double hiptoss and a double noggin knocker. Valentino ends T.C.F.'s offence with a trip on Mark and with a knee drives him to the outside. Mark spits at Valentino as Matt distracts the referee. "He fell," protests White. Valentino tags in White who connects with a corner clothesline and chops before tagging Valentino back in again. Matt hits White with a leg drop but Valentino breaks it up.

Matt follows up with a running DDT for another two count. A head scissors by Mark takes Valentino out of the ring, fireman's roll by Matt followed by a Senton of the top rope is enough for the 1, 2 and 3. The SWWA fans clap as The Clarke Foundation pose, The Emotional Express break into tears. "He hurt my face!" The crowd give them a sarcastic "awwwwwwwwwwww" as they leave.

Match Time: 13 minutes

Winners: The Clarke Foundation (Matt & Mark Clarke)

That was a good tag match. The Clarke Foundation showed me a lot of intensity (which I hadn't seen before) and gel well as a tag team. The Emotional Express work well together and have good characters that the fans love to hate. Good job by all four men as they put forth a good old school tag that the SWWA fans seemed to enjoy.

Poison vs British Born Steele with Special Guest Referee, Bodycount

Poison attacks BBS from behind, choking him with a chair and attempting to ram BBS's face into the steel steps but BBS reverses and its Poison who tastes the steel! BBS rolls Poison back in the ring and gets a quick two count. BBS follows up with a dropkick and another two count, a suplex and bulldog follow with both moves securing two counts. The crowd show their support for BBS with chants of, "BBS, BBS!" Poison reverses an Irish whip and connects with a clothesline. Northern lights/Perfect-plex combination by BBS gets another two count.

The follow up top rope splash misses, knee/bulldog combination by Poison allows him the advantage as he sets up for his TKO but BBS reverses into a Back-Cracker for the 1, 2 and 3. The fans clap for BBS as he leaves, BBS returns shortly after with a video camera (he shows Poison the footage) and then picks Poison up shaking hands with him.

Poison takes the microphone. "BBS, you've proved yourself and as SWWA owner, I'm making you #1 Contender for SWWA Championship!"

BBS thanks Poison and leaves.

Match Time: 9 minutes

Winner: British Born Steele

That was a very good match with a compelling storyline. I enjoyed the way BBS was all business trying to end the match as soon as he possibly could by attempting covers after a lot of moves in the early going and throughout the match. He knew deep down this match shouldn't have taken place, as he was accused of something he didn't do.

Poison performed well also and Bodycount called it right down the middle, I enjoyed the way BBS finally proved his innocence via the video camera. BBS vs The Bouncer should be a good match in its own right, when it takes place. I would have given this match the 10-11 minutes (I would personally have shaven off of Adams vs Icon) because with more time this match could have been great!

INTERMISSION

Hall Of Fame Induction

Poison calls Bodycount back out to the ring. Poison talks of how "It is an honour and privilege to call you a friend. We travelled all over the world (US, Dubai

& Wales!), I'm looking for a tag partner! What do you say Poison & Bodycount as a Tag Team!?" Bodycount and Poison shake hands.

Well that worked as well, I have never seen Bodycount wrestle but I'm intrigued by his and Poison's teaming in SWWA and wonder what will the future be for them in SWWA. Good segment.

Carnage w/Bacardi vs Shannon Hammer

Hammer ducks under Carnage's attempted clothesline and slaps him on the back. Carnage takes over Hammer with a headlock, Hammer quickly reverses out and with a shoulder block knocks Carnage down. Carnage connects with a hiptoss, Japanese armdrag and a leg lariat as the fans chant, "Carnage, Carnage!" Hammer leaves the ring and grabs Bacardi and uses her as a shield to cheap shot Carnage, Bacardi gets her own back by whipping Hammer.

Hammer misses a Senton off the top rope. "Carnage!" chants once more from the crowd, Carnage double chops Hammer and then connects with a spine buster. Transitioning into The Sharpshooter. "Tap," chant occurs directed towards Hammer, but Hammer manages to get to the ropes. Carnage uses the ropes for a powerbomb but that only manages a two count, Hammer hits back with a powerbomb of his own but with a follow up crossbody Carnage catches him and quickly connects with The Carnage-Bolt for the 1, 2 and 3.

Match Time: 11 minutes

Winner: Carnage w/Barcadi

That was a good match, much better performance from Carnage given the AWW match with Ronin a week earlier (proof that it was just a bad day for both men). Carnage summoned his cruiserweight powers in this match busting out a hurricanrana!

Hammer's cockiness in the early going seemed to have cost him in the end, Bacardi did what all good managers do support their Guy/Girl and lead them to victory, and she also proved she is no pushover when confronted by Hammer. Good match!

SWWA Tag Team Titles

John Bull & Aphrodite vs Mad Mike & Ronin (c)

Ronin and Mike eat sweets and then lock-up with each other! (With Ronin pushing Mike off). Ronin and Dite square off but Ronin is way too tall, Dite can't lock-up so she attempts a waistlock and a headlock but she is thrown off so she decides to make the tag to Bull. Bull puts Ronin in a full nelson and then connects with a DDT, Dite kicks Ronin and that distracts Mike. Powerslam by Ronin on Dite but Bull breaks it up leading to Bull and Ronin fighting.

Mike locks in the crossface but that is all broken up, Bull comes back with a spear. Carnage and Bacardi interfere as the referee is down, Bacardi hits a number of forearms on Dite and follows up with a facebuster allowing Mike to get the 1, 2 and 3. Mike takes Dite's head and shoves it into Ronin's ass, as the fans clap and cheer.

Match Time: 11 minutes

Winner and STILL SWWA Tag Team Champions: Mad Mike & Ronin (c)

That was a good comedy tag match, some of the wrestling was mistimed but on the whole didn't really detract from the match. Mike & Ronin's lock-up at the beginning was a laugh out loud moment!

Aphrodite looked ok in the exchanges she had with both men, but I still want to see her wrestle a woman before I can give a fair assessment of her wrestling skills. Bull performed well and all in all it was an enjoyable comedy tag match.

SWWA Championship

'The Messiah' Brandon Thomas vs The Bouncer w/The Boss (c)

Lock-up which Thomas gets the best of applying a wristlock to Bouncer, but Bouncer manages to reach the ropes. Thomas applies another wristlock and swings Bouncer around and to the mat. Thomas locks in the Fujiwara armbar. "Break his arm!" chant the fans, Bouncer escapes via a low blow to Thomas. Bouncer uses his fist and knee to scrape against Thomas and follows up with a sideslam for a two count. Thomas rallies and returns with a swinging slam and an elbow drop but Boss distracts him. Bouncer pushes Thomas back into the corner and follows up with a Northern lariat. "How dare you touch The Boss!"

Bouncer attempts to lift Thomas but he can't and falls to the mat with Thomas on top 1, 2 and 3! NEW

CHAMPION... well not quite although the fans saw Boss miss putting Bouncer's foot on the ropes the Ref didn't see it so the match is restarted. Bouncer is able to pick up Thomas this time and connects with his F-5 for the 1, 2 and 3. Thomas berates the Ref as the fans boo Bouncer.

Match Time: 13 minutes

Winner and STILL SWWA Champion: The Bouncer w/The Boss (c)

That was a good main event, and a good way to end the show! Bouncer and Thomas put forth two equally good performances and it made for a good match-up. Bouncer is a lucky man though (his foot was clearly not on the ropes), and with that Thomas has a definite cause for a rematch. One that I'm sure he will take up at some point down the line in SWWA.

TGR and Tucker opened the show with a good back and forth match, Hall Of Fame segments worked well, Adams vs Icon was good although a bit long. Clarke Foundation vs Emotional Express was a good solid tag team affair, BBS vs Poison was my match of the night as it encapsulated everything wrestling needs (good wrestling, intensity, a good storyline and definitive conclusion). Carnage vs Hammer was another good match with intensity and cruiserweight Carnage!

SWWA Tag Team Titles match was good, based on the comedy involved and Bouncer vs Thomas was a good way to end the show and screw job like finish should lead to a rematch, which I would like to see. SWWA has the potential to be a good promotion (in their own right) if they can just put wrongs (which I have discussed in the report) right.

Match of the Night:
British Born Steele vs Poison

October 2007 Thoughts

My Live Match of October 2007:
45 Minute Iron Man Match for 1PW Openweight Title

Darren Burridge vs Nigel McGuinness (c) (1PW 2nd Year Anniversary 13th October 2007)

My Live Show of October 2007:
Anti-Watershed Wrestling (25th October 2007)

12. NOVEMBER 2007

Future Championship Wrestling

Date: Saturday 10th November 2007
Time: 7:00pm
Attendance: 360
Price: General - £10 or a Party of 4 - £36
Location: The Glades Arena, Kidderminster, West Midlands.

Kris Godsize welcomes the crowd to FCW 'Anarchy at The Arena,' he also has the unfortunate task of telling the fans that Sterling James Keenan's flight was delayed and he won't be here.

Battle Royal for Match vs 'Dark Angel' Carl Mizzery

The Hunter Brothers (Lee & Jim) vs Lord Graham Thomas vs Jay Icon vs The Masked Inferno vs 'Star Man' Mark Clarke vs 'Red Tiger' Axel Bowen vs B52 vs 'Ladies Favourite' Damien Grant vs Blade

Icon tries to eliminate LGT but only receives chops for his trouble.
    Quick eliminations follow as Jim Hunter, Mark Clarke, Masked Inferno & Lee Hunter are thrown out. Icon low bridges B52 sending him out of the ring, Blade follows shortly after (eliminated by Bowen). A big boot by LGT eliminates Grant from the Battle Royal.
    Leaving three men in the ring (LGT, Icon & Bowen) Bowen & LGT double team Icon with chops.

Icon fights back with an avalanche splash on LGT & Bowen in the corner knocking Bowen and LGT down in a compromising position!

LGT holds Icon but he manages to move causing Bowen to connect with a clothesline on LGT and with that Icon throws LGT out.

It's now one on one between Icon and Bowen for a match with Mizzery, Icon takes control with a clothesline/bulldog combination but can't eliminate Bowen. Bowen recovers with a rake to the eyes, Icon returns with a top rope clothesline. He is distracted by FCW Champion Saul Adams (c) and that is enough to allow Bowen to pick up the win by bundling Icon out.

Match Time: 7 minutes

Winner: 'Red Tiger' Axel Bowen

Aftermath:

Adams and Bowen continue the beat down on Icon until Doug Williams and the FCW locker room interject, Williams asks, "What kind of Champion are you?" (after attacking Icon 2 on 1) and challenges Adams to an FCW Title match tonight. Adams accepts. Williams turns to the crowd and states, "I'm going to take the FCW Title Belt off that coward!"

The fans start a "Loser" chant directed at Adams and clap as Williams leaves.

Well that was rushed! 7 minutes given to a Battle Royal involving 10 men was strange and led to a pretty nothing contest as it was mostly blink and you'll miss it eliminations.

One man looked good in the Battle Royal and that man was Jay Icon who showed a great intensity and had the fans support in his losing effort. The Battle Royal's job was to find a new opponent for Carl Mizzery and that was achieved as Axel Bowen won the match.

'Second Coming' Celt Kennedy vs 'Wonderkid' Jonny Storm

Pre-Match:
Kennedy takes the microphone. "Time for all you brats to go back to your seats!" A kid tries to talk up. "Can't understand what you're saying loser, sit down and shut up or go home." Kennedy then turns his attention to Storm. "This loser represents all of you people!" Kennedy then challenges the fans. Joel 'Afro' Allen (the Referee) has heard enough and swipes the mic away.

Match:
Lock-up with Kennedy gaining control pushing Storm into the corner when the Ref asks for a clean break he slaps Storm's chest. Storm wins the second lock-up and pushes Kennedy into the corner, on the clean break Kennedy punches Storm in the face. The fans chant "Jonny, Jonny" Kennedy wins a third lock-up but his punch is blocked and Storm fires back with some of his own. Kennedy flips Storm into the air, Storm positions himself and hits with the hurricanrana and with a follow up low bridge Kennedy finds himself out of the ring.

Storm hits with his patented top rope Japanese Armdrag. "6-1-9!" chant starts up but Storm is reversed whipped and Kennedy levels him with a spear for a two count. Kennedy struggles to the top rope and misses the subsequent Senton. Storm quickly follows up with a dropkick landing Kennedy on the middle rope and connects with a 6-1-9, Kennedy falls in position and Storm hits with a jump up moonsault from the second rope for the 1, 2 and 3.

Match Time: 15 minutes

Winner: 'Wonderkid' Jonny Storm

That was a good match. Kennedy who I had not seen before impressed me with his wrestling skills and his jawing with the crowd was hilarious at times.

Storm brought his fast paced style to Kidderminster and it meshed well with Kennedy leading to a match the FCW fans enjoyed. A good solid wrestling match by both men.

ROH vs FCW

Jimmy Jacobs vs The Bouncer

The fans chant, "Bouncer, Bouncer!"

Jacobs complains, "I'm an international superstar!"

The fans chant "Yankee, Yankee," at him. As Bouncer enters Jacobs leaves causing the fans to chant "Chicken!" at him.

"I'm not a chicken" Jacobs retorts. Lock-up Jacobs ducks out and leaves the ring once more, the FCW fans chant and clap for Bouncer. Jacobs returns stating he needs complete silence to wrestle.

Headlock by Bouncer who quickly transitions into a wristlock. "Should I break it?" he asks the crowd, Jacobs puts his foot on the ropes to break the hold. "Chicken!" chants once more.

Bouncer calls for the F-5 but Jacobs gets out and connects with a spear for a two count, Jacobs continues the attack with a Texas Cloverleaf but Bouncer struggles his way to the ropes

Jacobs climbs the turnbuckle and jumps off with a Senton but Bouncer gets his knees up, Jacobs attempts his finishing move the Contra Code but Bouncer skilfully catches Jacobs and turns it into an F-5 for the 1, 2 and 3.

Match Time: 15 minutes

Winner: The Bouncer

That was another good match, back and forth with chances for either man to win. Jacobs played the coward to perfection as the chants of "Chicken" signify, Bouncer went toe to toe with Jacobs wrestling wise also and looked impressive.

The match had wrestling, brawling, crowd interaction and a tremendous finish (with Bouncer reversing the Contra Code into the F-5) to pick up a huge upset win, and in doing so proved to any doubters that he is indeed the real deal.

INTERMISSION

Kris Godsize announces that FCW will be back at The Glades Arena on March 8th 2008.

Three Way Tag Team match for FCW Tag Team Titles

Swift Justice ('Bird of Prey' Falcon & The Judge) vs Gunns of Steele (Tommy Gunn & British Born Steele) vs Pl4Y ('The Messiah' Brandon Thomas & Kev O'Neil w/Kelli) (c)

The kids at ringside fight over the plastic gun Tommy brought to the ring! Gunns of Steele dropkick both teams out of the ring, but they quickly return and put a beat down on G.O.S. but G.O.S. fight back with dropkicks and then try a double leap frog but Gunn mistimes his and gets caught by Falcon. Pl4y beat on G.O.S. until they manage to fight back with stereo hurricanranas to take Pl4y to the outside, BBS follows up with a slingshot body splash.

Judge hits Gunn with a back suplex and Falcon quickly follows up with a top rope leg drop for a two count. Falcon applies a nerve hold on Gunn as the fans clap, he sarcastically states, "All of you are clapping for me."

BBS has seen enough and runs at Falcon who hastily exits the ring. "You should show me the respect I deserve!" he tells the FCW fans. Falcon follows up with a DVD on Gunn but once again can only get a two count. Falcon gets frustrated and tries to get a pinfall anyway he can with a number of consecutive falls in the next minute or so, but to no avail.

Thomas knees Gunn and follows up with a club to his back, BBS interrupts with a Backcracker on Thomas allowing Gunn to hit a Senton on Thomas, Kelli interferes grabbing BBS by the hair. This allows Falcon to hit the Kryptonite Crunch on BBS, Thomas connects with a low blow on Falcon and throws him out of the ring, before pinning BBS for the 1, 2 and 3.

Match Time: 22 minutes

Winners and STILL FCW Tag Team Champions: Pl4Y ('The Messiah' Brandon Thomas & Kev O'Neil w/Kelli) (c)

That was a good old school tag team match to kick off the second half of the show. All three teams looked impressive as the match progressed, Gunn took a hell of a beating but showed his incredible resilience by fighting back and finally tagging in BBS.
    Swift Justice looked solid and garnered a bit of hatred from the crowd, Pl4y proved to be the opportunists with the quick and cheap pinfall that ended the match. Another good match on a solid card thus far.

'Red Tiger' Axel Bowen vs 'Dark Angel' Carl Mizzery

Bowen endears himself to the FCW fans: "Chance to prove yourself, you little freaks!" during a posing match which Mizzery won, the fans even asked Bowen, "Who are ya?"
    Bowen attacks Mizzery from behind, Irish whipping Mizzery but Mizzery leapfrogs over and takes Bowen down with a hiptoss and dropkick. Mizzery kicks Bowen's leg and follows with a

standing moonsault, Bowen rolls out. "In the ring!" shouts Mizzery.

Bowen retorts, "I'll get in the ring when I'm good and ready." Mizzery levels Bowen with a T-Bone suplex as the fans clap, Mizzery then jumps from the mat to the top rope but misses with his attempted splash. Bowen takes advantage and connects with a Blackhole slam for a close nearfall, he can't believe that hasn't ended the match. Bowen pushes Mizzery in the corner and fights with him on the turnbuckle, Mizzery pushes Bowen off and hits with a Frog splash for the 1, 2 and 3 to a loud cheer from the FCW fans.

Match Time: 12 minutes

Winner: 'Dark Angel' Carl Mizzery

It was a disappointment that Sterling James Keenan's flight was delayed, but this match was another good one and in the end I don't think Keenan was missed that much (based on it).

Bowen and Mizzery wrestled a pretty even contest as they both looked for ways to put their opponent away, it looked all over with the Blackhole slam but Mizzery fought back and showed his high flying skills ending the match with a Frog splash. Good match!

FCW Championship

'The Anarchist' Doug Williams vs 'New Sensation' Saul Adams (c)

Pre-Match:
Adams tells the fans to "Shut their little mouths." Bowen sneaks up behind Williams and smacks him in the back with a chair (before the bell has rang), Adams follows up by ramming Williams's head into two separate steel ringposts and after choking Williams finally rolls him in and with that the match starts.

Match:
Adams goes straight for the pin but can only get a two count, Adams connects with a backbreaker for a two once again, frustrated he tells the Ref to count faster. Bowen comes into the ring as Adams holds Williams but Williams moves and Bowen boots Adams, Williams follows up with a clothesline for a two count. Williams continues the offence with punches and a hiptoss before applying the wristlock and hitting an armbreaker, Adams is able to reverse out with a snapmere and headlock but Williams skilfully reverses out of the headlock and back into a wristlock of his own.

Adams connects with a Blue thunder bomb and definitely gets a three count from the Referee with the bell ringing, but the Referee states he made a mistake and the match is restarted. Adams and the Ref argue over the count, Bowen throws a steel chair in but Williams is wise to it and hits Bowen with a spinebuster on the chair. Williams looks all set for the win when he attempts the Chaos Theory on Adams but Adams low blows Williams and Bowen gives him another for good measure. Adams once again connects with a Blue thunder bomb for the 1, 2 and 3.

Post-Match:
The fans boo Adams and Bowen, Williams comes to and gets a measure of revenge with a double noggin knocker on the two men. Williams follows up with a clothesline on Adams and takes possession of the FCW Heavyweight Title, the fans clap for Williams as he leaves.

Match Time: 15 minutes

Winner and STILL FCW Champion: 'New Sensation' Saul Adams (c)

That was a good main event, and a good way to end the show! Williams and Adams put forth good performances in a match that had run-ins, scientific wrestling, cheating, the Ref being knocked down and finally a pretty cheap finish.

The cheap finish was ok though because the wrestling that had gone before it was of a good standard, the way the match ended it looks like Williams vs Adams 2 could happen shortly and I'm all for that.

Jay Icon looked impressive in the throw away Battle Royal to start the show. Kennedy and Storm put forth a good match, Bouncer matched ROH Star Jimmy Jacobs in the match of the night, the 3 way tag was a good old school match, Mizzery & Bowen contested a back and forth match and Williams vs Adams was a good match to end the show.

FCW came to Kidderminster with an impressive card and even minus Sterling James Keenan delivered a night of good wrestling from start to finish to a crowd of 360 people which is an impressive feat in its own right.

Match of the Night:
Jimmy Jacobs vs The Bouncer

Extreme 2 Wrestling

Date: Friday 23rd November 2007
Time: 7:30pm
Attendance: 27 (Including Spud and Dave Moralez)
Price: £5
Location: Quarry Bank Community Centre, Sheffield Street, Quarry Bank, West Midlands DY5 2AA.

Kris Godsize welcomes the crowd to E2W.

'The Mad Man from Japan' Wedow Wonchow vs Geraden (w/Corri)

Lock-up with Wonchow transitioning into the headlock on Geraden, Geraden reverses out and rakes Wonchow's head on the ropes. Geraden follows up with a suplex on Wonchow as Corri distracts the Referee handing Geraden the whip (she carried to the ring). Wonchow steals the whip and whips Corri's ass and throws the whip back at Geraden! Corri believes Geraden whipped her and chases him around the ring, Geraden runs into Wonchow who suplexes him and manages to get the 3 count.

Match Time: 4 minutes

Winner: 'The Mad Man from Japan' Wedow Wonchow

WOW! That was a blink and you might miss it match. Geraden showed he is more than a good wrestler, because of his working on a good character also. Wonchow was hilarious as was the match, nice sequence with who whipped Corri but a suplex ending a match made Geraden look pretty weak.

LGT vs The Bouncer

LGT ducks out of The Bouncer's lock-up attempts, and heads to the back. The crowd breaks out with a chant of "Chicken" LGT barely makes it back to the ring before the 10 count (returning on 9). After breaking the count LGT takes a seat at ringside, Bouncer has seen enough and follows before throwing LGT back in. LGT punches Bouncer and then begs off as Bouncer looks to extract revenge. LGT was playing possum though and quickly throws Bouncer into the steel ringpost.

LGT stands on both of Bouncer's hands, Bouncer returns with a low blow, knocking both men down as the fans clap. Bouncer follows up with a powerslam and a leg drop for a two count, Bouncer kicks LGT square in the face! Before attempting the F-5, LGT skilfully reverses looking for a stunner but Bouncer rolls through into a pin for the 1, 2 and 3.

Match Time: 11 minutes

Winner: The Bouncer

That was a good match. LGT played the coward role well, and the fans were firmly behind The Bouncer with everything he did. This transpired into a good wrestling match as both men looked like they were one big move away from the win, in this case a skilful pin by The Bouncer ended the match.

3-Some (Dan Ryder & Danny Devine w/Miss Ryder) vs The Dutt-Lee Boyz ('Sik' Nik Dutt & Chandler Scott Lee)

Ryder and Dutt lock-up with Ryder easily able to push Dutt down, before tagging out to Devine whilst Dutt tags CSL. Devine puts an Apple in his mouth but drops it as the bigger CSL enters, CSL pushes Devine off after a lock-up. Picking up the Apple before bowling it into both Devine and Ryders crotches! CSL Irish whips Devine and with a follow up splash Devine and Ryder end up a compromising position.

The fans chant, "3D, 3D!" CSL hits Devine with an elbow drop. Ryder grabs CSL's hair pulling him down to the mat. Ryder then attacks Dutt on the outside, Miss Ryder distracts CSL long enough for Devine to roll him up and with his feet on the ropes, manages to pick up the pinfall.

Post-Match:
Dutt chases Ryder back into the ring and then he and CSL hit the 3D as the fans go crazy! Following up with one to Devine for good measure.

"Whaaaaaaaaaaaaatsup!" follows as the fans cheer.

Match Time: 15 minutes

Winners: 3-Some (Dan Ryder & Danny Devine w/Miss Ryder)

That was a good old school tag team match! What happens when you take two of the best wrestlers in the UK and give them good characters? MONEY for whichever promotion decide to book them of course, that is how I would sum up 3-Some.

Dutt and Lee worked well as a team and 3-Some bring antics and good wrestling skill to any match they are in, this produced a good match which the E2W fans enjoyed.

INTERMISSION

Jay Icon (w/Aphrodite) vs 'The Rock' Ashton Maivia

Moralez feigns throwing a cup of tea at Icon, Icon gets scared and cowers away. Headlock by Icon, who quickly follows with punches, Ashton fights back with punches and a spit punch sends Icon over the top rope to the floor. Ashton follows and quickly whips Icon into the crowd, Icon returns by whipping Ashton into a wall! Ashton connects with a spine-buster before taking off his elbow pad for the people's elbow, which he hits but can only get a two count.

Ashton attempts a Rock Bottom but Icon cleverly reverses into a Stunner for the 1, 2 and 3. LGT spits Beer in Icon's face. Icon challenges LGT to go outside, LGT walks out the door. Icon changes his mind and walks to the back. The fans chant "Rocky" as Ashton returns to his feet.

Match Time: 7 minutes

Winner: Jay Icon w/Aphrodite

That was a good match! Back and forth contest which could have gone either way, Ashton's 'Rock' mannerisms were spot on and added a lot to the match.

   Icon put forth a good performance in his own right and with that combination, a good match transpired. The ending was much like that of Stone Cold Steve Austin vs The Rock from Wrestlemania 15 and it worked well.

Tucker vs Psycho

Duelling chants of, "Psycho/Tucker!" start this match, Tucker nips up after being knocked down by Psycho. Tucker shoulder blocks Psycho down and then they mirror each other's moves with none of them connecting because they are being done at the same exact time! Standoff between the two competitors as the fans clap, Psycho follows up with a powerslam.

   The two wrestlers then shake hands but Tucker uses this as opportunity to put Psycho in a headlock. Psycho connects with a suplex on Tucker but Tucker rolls through and almost steals the win (two count only), kick by Tucker who follows up with a springboard but Psycho expertly catches him in an armbar and somersaults over into a pin for the 1, 2 and 3.

Match Time: 6 minutes

Winner: Psycho

Good back and forth match for the time allowed. Tucker plays the cocky but skilful wrestler well, Psycho had the hometown support and at times that allowed him to control the match. I have never seen a finish to a match like a somersault from an armbar into a pinfall that was AMAZING!

Dr. X vs British Born Steele

Pre-Match:
Dr X leaves and runs around the ring, before touching his toes. When the match seems scheduled to go ahead, BBS does the same as both men traded off warm up exercises.

Match:
Lock-up which BBS reverses out into a wristlock and then the two competitors trade wristlocks. BBS ends the sequence by dropkicking X and with a follow up DDT manages a two count. X rakes BBS's eyes and kicks him in the head before quickly following up with a chop for a two count. X blocks the turnbuckle and connects with the dreaded stomp, BBS fights back with forearms and chops. A snapmere follows with kicks to the chest of X.

X tells the crowd that he has had enough of beating BBS's ass and challenges him to a dance off! He hilariously asks for the music guy "Put some Michael Jackson on!" The crowd cheer for X and clap and cheer for BBS, as they are X attacks BBS from behind. A "B, B, B, B, B, S!" chant starts up! BBS fights out with forearms as the fans clap, X returns with a knee to the face and a lariat for a close nearfall. BBS regains his composure and from out of nowhere hits an RKO for the 1, 2 and 3.

Post-Match:
The fans cheer and chant, "BBS, BBS!" and "One more match!" X takes the microphone. "This ring, same place, some time. BBS vs Dr X 2!"

Match Time: 15 minutes

Winner: British Born Steele

That was a good main event, and a good way to end the show! Dr X and BBS brought Comedy and good wrestling to the main event of the evening, trading holds in the early going, before X's cheating turned the match.

The dance-off is always fun to see and added more hilarity to the match, the ending sequence was well done with both men mere seconds away from ending the match before BBS's RKO did just that!

Wonchow is as crazy as his name seems, Geraden is working on a good character. LGT and Bouncer wrestled a competitive match, 3-Some vs Dutt-Lee Boyz was a good old school tag match. Icon vs Ashton was a good comedy/wrestling match.

Psycho vs Tucker was good while it lasted with a wicked finish! Dr X vs BBS was laugh out loud funny for the entire time it took place! A good match in its own right with great crowd interaction, dance-off and good wrestling.

E2W does have its problems though, the ring was pretty much like a double sized bed! 20 + people paying to watch a show is pretty ludicrous as well, pure wrestling fans would have despised this show.

Causal wrestling fans would have found another reason to laugh at Pro Wrestling but for the people looking for a good night out at a fun wrestling show this was superb and for entertainment I haven't laughed so much being at a wrestling show in my entire 16 years as a fan!

Match of the Night:
Dr X vs British Born Steele

Legends Wrestling League

Date: Tuesday 27th November 2007
Time: 7:30pm
Attendance: 70
Price: Adults £5, £4 with LWL Flyer (Downloadable from http://www.lwluk.co.uk) Kids £3.
Location: Legends Members Club, Oxley Street, Wolverhampton, West Midlands, WV1 1QN.

Motor Mouth Mike is your Ring Announcer for this evening.

Joey Syxx vs Kris Navarro

Both men shake hands in a great sign of sportsmanship. Navarro takes control of the opening lock-up by applying the wristlock to Syxx, Syxx reverses out and Navarro reverses back in using the ropes for leverage. Syxx uses Navarro's momentum against him and reverses into a wristlock of his own. The bigger man Navarro knocks Syxx down with a shoulder block, Syxx and Navarro then battle over who will get hiptossed. Navarro wins the battle and quickly follows with an armdrag and Japanese armdrag for good measure.

Syxx connects with a top rope FrankenSteiner off the top rope putting both men down, as the Ref begins the obligatory 10 count, the fans clap. Chops are traded as both men return to their feet, Navarro misses with his patented Enzuguri. Syxx returns with a German suplex but misses with the follow up Frog splash, Navarro calls for a 'Spear' but misses. Syxx fights back but as he attempts a kick Navarro catches him with the Spear and the pinfall is academic from there. Both men shake hands as the fans clap.

Match Time: 7 minutes

Winner: Kris Navarro

When I looked at the card I wondered why Navarro was wrestling in the opening match against a wrestler from the LWL academy (no disrespect meant to Syxx) but I felt Navarro deserved better. Syxx showed some promise, but also looked a little rough around the edges mid-match but that is something I'm sure he can improve on, not a bad showing for the first time I've seen him. Navarro wrestled a very good match in his own right and looked to be better than this match.

'Mr #1' Jonny Costello w/'Hellbunny' Vicky Morton vs Chandler Scott Lee

Mike introduces Costello in an American accent much to delight of the fans, who laughed outrageously! Costello retorts, "I'm not some kind of comedy act! Goofy!" He then berates a female in the crowd. "That's the worst impression of a woman I have ever seen!"

CSL pushes Costello back into the corner, Costello bellows, "Get him back!" CSL applies a wristlock whilst doing Dude Love struts. Costello reverses out into an armbar, CSL reverses once more into a wristlock. Morton throws the Confederate flag in the ring and distracts the Ref, Costello connects with a couple of flag shots.

CSL fights back and connects with a fameasser but Costello manages to get his foot on the rope for the break. CSL attempts a second fameasser but misses allowing Costello to hit with a full nelson slam for the 3 count.

Match Time: 7 minutes

Winner: 'Mr #1' Jonny Costello w/'Hellbunny' Vicky Morton

A decent match added to the card, but much like CSL vs TGR last month I wouldn't have missed it had it been left off the card. With no disrespect meant to either competitor, with 7 other matches and possible over-run to contend with this match probably should have been taken off the card.

With that being said it wasn't a bad match, both men worked hard. Nice chain wrestling at the start,

Costello cheating towards the end, CSL missing that 'big' move and Costello hitting his to end the match.

Mad Dog Maxx vs Tommy Gunn

Pre-Match:
Maxx shouts, "Shut your stinking mouths up!" and barks scaring the Ref! A member of the audience hilariously adds, "Don't look at me I DON'T fancy you!" At this point Maxx is seething. The fans chant, "Tommy Gunn, Tommy Gunn!" as Gunn makes his long awaited return to an LWL ring. Maxx barks again scaring the Ref once more.

Match:
Maxx attacks Gunn from behind, punching him in the head. "Shut your stinking mouths up!" he berates the crowd. Gunn fights back with a headscissors and calls for a 6-1-9 but Maxx rolls out of the ring telling the fans, "You are not going to see the 6-1-9."

The fans retort with, "You need putting down!" Maxx climbs on the ringside table and paces up and down. "Tell him to get back Ref!" Maxx shouts, Gunn starts a chant of, "Chicken!"

Maxx retorts, "I'll show you a Chicken."

Gunn leapfrogs Maxx landing him in the perfect position for the 6-1-9 which he connects with but only manages a two count! Which Gunn questions the Ref for, he then calls for the top rope but misses the follow up Splash. Maxx returns with a vicious lariat and whilst holding the tights the match is all over! The fans boo Maxx and chant "Mad Dog sucks," Maxx intimidates the fans, the fans clap for Gunn as he returns to his feet.

Match Time: 12 minutes

Winner: Mad Dog Maxx

Good match! It's great to see Gunn back in an LWL ring as he brings something unique to the table. Maxx has the best character in the company and has the wrestling skills to back it up. Both competitors worked hard in a pretty back and forth match that could have gone either way.

Gunn missed the splash and Maxx hit the lariat and with that the match was done! With Maxx pulling the tights to win, Gunn has a legitimate claim for a rematch at some point down the road and that is a match I would love to see.

LWL National Pride Championship

Mr. Valentino vs Dan Ryder (c)

Pre-Match:
"On your knees and bow down before me!" Valentino shouts, to which a kid takes a swipe at Valentino! "I'm in the perfect state of mind to destroy Dan Ryder." Ryder enters to much fanfare which riles Valentino causing him to attack from behind.

Actually slamming Ryder's head (and yes I do mean head) into the wooden tables at ringside! Causing the fans to shout "oooooooooooh" and "aaaaaaaaaah" as they fear for Ryder's safety.

"His head is as thick as mine," gloats Valentino, Ryder blocks the ringpost and slams Valentino.

Match:
Both competitors trade chops with Ryder's sounding like a gunshot! Valentino counters with Kobashi-like chops, Ryder throws him out over the top rope. Ryder asks the fans, "Who wants to chop Valentino?" and then allows those who said yes to do just that (including Carnage). Ryder throws Valentino back in and quickly continues the attack with a corner 10 punch. Ryder continues with forearms and feigns one causing Valentino to fall, Ryder jokingly asks, "Did I just touch him?" and follows up with a northern lights suplex for a two count.

With Ryder in control he attempts his patented split leg twisting moonsault but as he turns the ropes seem to be loose and he lands directly on his HEAD! Somehow he manages to continue to the relief of every fan in the Legends Members Club. Valentino takes advantage of the situation and quickly locks in the Sharpshooter with audible screams from Ryder, he somehow manages to reach the ropes, Valentino pulls him back to mid-ring but Ryder's fortitude is a sight to behold as he reaches the ropes once more.

Valentino leaves the ring for a chair, as he is about to hit Ryder the Ref grabs the chair. Unfortunately for Ryder the Ref struggles to remove the chair from the ring, so Valentino steals the LWL National Pride Title and levels with Ryder with it! It's over... NO! Ryder gets his shoulder up on the 2 and 9/10's count!! Valentino berates the Ref before wailing on Ryder with forearms, Ryder returns with a vicious slap and a head butt!

Ryder proving he is indeed a crazy individual heads up top once more and connects with a picture perfect 450 splash for the pinfall! As the fans cheer loudly, Valentino moans, "I want my belt!" and throws a temper tantrum before stating, "I'm going to get MY belt at the next show!"

Match Time: 17 minutes

Winner and STILL LWL National Pride Champion: Dan Ryder (c)

That was a great match! Ryder and Valentino showed chemistry in the awesome tag match last month (Tagging with Marcus Kool and Danny Devine respectively), this was a fine one on one match between the two. Ryder is a crazy individual and truly gives his all for the fans, from literally having his head SLAMMED off the wooden tables to recovering from falling on his HEAD!

Valentino has a tremendous character one which the fans love to hate, a mixture of the both led to a great match which left the LWL fans in awe! This match was a last minute replacement because Devine couldn't be there and next month will be the four way that was scheduled between Ryder vs Valentino vs Devine vs Kool and I for one can't wait!

INTERMISSION

The Bouncer w/The Boss vs Marcus Kool

Kool fires off a back elbow and dropkick knocking Bouncer out of the ring. Chops follow before Kool throws Bouncer back in. Kool is in control until Boss grabs his leg as he runs at the ropes. Bouncer then attacks Kool from behind and hits a powerslam but only manages a one count. Bouncer continues the assault by choking Kool on the ropes and when he leaves Boss continues choking Kool. Bouncer then boots away at Kool.

Bouncer attempts the F-5 but Kool skilfully reverses it into a DDT and climbs the ropes, Boss distracts Kool but Kool kicks him off, unfortunately he misses with the Senton. Bouncer feels the match is over and wants to put an exclamation point on it with an F-5 amazingly Kool reverses out once more this time into a Superkick for the 3 count.

Match Time: 12 minutes

Winner: Marcus Kool

Good match! Which got the crowd quickly back into the show after Intermission, both competitors performed well and that transpired into an enjoyable match for the LWL fans to bear witness to.
Both men controlled different parts of the match leading to a back and forth contest which either man could have won. I really was left in AWE at the finish to the match as never in a million years did I think an F-5 could be reversed into a Superkick!

'Mr New Age' Kristian 'The Flame' Lees:

The fans greet Lees with chants of, "Who are ya?"
Lees retorts, "I'll keep my questions short and sweet otherwise it will take you two weeks to answer! Did you enjoy Kris Navarro vs Joey Syxx?" The fans cheer, Lees wasn't impressed. "Best of The Academy, what a joke!" Fans boo loudly. "It's a

matter of respect, that I'm not getting!" Carnage, who was sitting in the crowd, has heard enough!

Fans cheer loudly as he enters the ring. "You think you're Tucker!" Lees slaps Carnage, Carnage returns with a number of vicious chops and a lariat. Lees rolls out and to the back, as Carnage announces, "Me and You next month in a Respect Match!" The fans cheer and chant, "Carnage, Carnage!" as he leaves.

Good promo by Kristian Lees, I wanted to see him wrestle since last month. So getting to see him wrestle Carnage next month should be a real test for the young competitor. Carnage answering Lees was a good move by LWL as he is one of the veteran wrestlers in the locker room. Carnage vs Lees should be a good match and when all is said and done you will be able to see if Lees can live up to the hype he has built for himself.

#1 Contendership Match for National Pride Championship

Platinum Paige vs Caiman

Paige professes that Wolverhampton is his town and the people love him, of course the fans boo him! Paige attacks Caiman from behind, Caiman has too much strength for Paige and easily pushes him off. Paige returns with a clothesline and after an elbow rolls out of the ring. Caiman follows and the chase is on, Caiman feigns getting in causing Paige to drop an elbow on canvas! Caiman follows up with a dropkick.

Paige connects with his patented Impaler but Caiman put his foot on the ropes and defiantly shouts "Screw your move!" Paige upset goes back to choking Caiman with his boot. Caiman fires back with chops and attempts a top rope splash which misses, Paige follows up quickly with a roll up pin with his feet on the ropes for the three count. Paige tells Caiman, "Go back to Wales!" and tells the fans how the LWL National Pride Title is all his.

Match Time: 9 minutes

Winner and NEW #1 Contender to LWL National Pride Championship: Platinum Paige

Ok match! Nothing too spectacular that set this match apart from the others on the card. Paige's character development is there for all to see and his wrestling skills are reaching the same level.

It was good to see a predominantly Welsh wrestling show wrestler make the trip to England for this show. Paige vs Ryder should be a good match if Ryder can survive four way next month. I'd like to see Caiman back at some point in the future also.

Sykes vs 'Sik' Nik Dutt

Pre-Match:
"You spend your hard earned dole money to come and watch me!" Sykes bellows. "I am a Pro Wrestler and I am in no fit state to compete, so the match is cancelled. I'm sparing you an ass kicking, Nik!"

The fans shout, "Exterminate!"

Sykes continues berating the crowd with pretty strong terms! Sykes climbs out of the ring to confront a fan, "I'll knock your teeth down your throat!"

Dutt enters and makes his way to the ring, Sykes tells Dutt to leave so he can win by Count-Out. Dutt hesitates and Sykes replies with, "The longer you are in this ring the more you'll annoy me."

Dutt finally leaves but at 9 runs back in and pushes Sykes!

Match:
Chops by Dutt as both men are on the outside. Dutt then throws Sykes into the crowd (unfortunately in this situation I am the crowd and Sykes lands right on top of me!) Sykes returns with a vicious club and throws Dutt back in the ring. A lariat follows by Sykes and a roll up pin for a two count. Dutt fires back with armdrags, continuing the momentum he connects with a dropkick and a wheelbarrow bulldog for a two count.

"No one clapping you, Nik!" Dutt jumps off the ropes straight into an RKO by Sykes for another two count. Sykes removes the straps scaring the Ref, "I no longer care about this match!" he shouts before low blowing Dutt, closed fists follow as well as vicious crossfaces. The final straw is when the Ref is knocked down, he finally throws the match out and awards it to Dutt via a DQ.

Post-Match:

Kris Navarro and Joey Syxx come down to the ring to stop Sykes. Sykes levels Syxx with a short-arm clothesline before being speared by Navarro (to a loud cheer from the LWL fans!) Sykes and Navarro square off, and come to blows trading forearms. Sykes. "I don't give a damn about you (Syxx) or you (Dutt) I want you! (Navarro)."

Fans chant, "TLC!" Sykes retorts with, "You probably don't know how to spell TLC!" before looking at Navarro. "Forget the rules, I'm going to beat the living hell out of you!" Sykes leaves after sharing a few choice words with LWL promoter.

Match Time: 11 minutes

Winner by Disqualification: 'Sik' Nik Dutt

WOW that was intense! If Sykes was annoyed in previous matches, man has he turned it up even further now. Sykes and Dutt kicked seven bells out of each other in a vicious brawl which I was unwontedly a part of! I believed Sykes wouldn't wrestle and he might face Dutt next month as time was ticking, but to my surprise Sykes showed not only can he wrestle clinics but he can brawl with the very best.

Dutt's stock rose in this match also as he was able to hang with one of the best in the UK, the DQ may have been a sour ending for some but it showed Sykes's do not care attitude to its maximum. Post-match was the real talking point, after waiting two months (although it seemed like longer)!

LWL is finally giving the fans what they have been begging to see (myself included) Kris Navarro vs Sykes 2! I truly cannot wait for the next show as if the second match is half as good as the first it should be one hell of a match!

LWL Championship

Matt Vaughn vs Mat Mensa (c)

Pre-Match:
Vaughn endears himself to the LWL fans by spraying water on them! Official ring introductions take place before the match starts.

Match:
Vaughn pushes Mensa back into the turnbuckle and chops him before breaking, Mensa does the same second time around to chants of, "Let's go, Mensa." The fans chant, "England!" at Vaughn who originates from Wales, Mensa misses a club but doesn't miss with a spinebuster which plants Vaughn. Vaughn is then hung upside down in the corner, Mensa follows up with a dropkick. Vaughn fires back and attempts to Press Mensa but Mensa fights out and with a dropkick sends Vaughn to the outside.

T-Bone suplex by Mensa and with a kick to Vaughn's mid-section an underhook suplex follows. Mensa going for Taz's Title of Human Suplex Machine follows up with a northern lights suplex for a two count. Vaughn reverses an Irish whip into a Samoan drop and quickly follows with a top rope elbow for a two count. Unhappy with cadence of the count he berates the Ref this leaves him open to Mensa's Perfect-plex for the 3 count.

Post-Match:
Mad Dog Maxx appears, singling for Mensa's LWL Title. "My belt," Maxx continues. "Don't know when I'm coming, but I'm coming, that Belt's mine!"

Mensa retorts, "I am still champ, calls Maxx a Ram-scallion, next month I am going to kill him and pin him 1, 2, 3!"

The fans break out in an, "LWL, LWL!" chant as the show ends.

Match Time: 14 minutes

Winner and STILL LWL Champion: Mat Mensa (c)

A decent main event, solid match from both competitors. Mensa is growing from strength to strength as LWL Champion, going from being least likely to hold the Title to being the only man for the job as of now. Vaughn looked ok in his LWL debut, much like the match a solid performance from Vaughn.

I saw Vaughn have a very good match with Justin Johnson at Celtic Wrestling so I'm guessing a clash of styles between he and Mensa stopped this match from being good upwards. Mensa vs Maxx should be a very good match come next month and I hope to see Vaughn back in LWL at some point in the future to show what he truly capable of!

I thought opening match was a waste of Navarro, but it turned out to be a decent match. Costello vs CSL was a match that didn't really click for whatever reason. Maxx vs Gunn was high impact and high paced and the ending was brutal! Ryder vs Valentino was a superb match that was well worth the overextended wait and is only just beaten by the amazing tag the two contested (along with Marcus Kool & Danny Devine last month). Bouncer vs Kool was a good match with a wicked ending!

Kristian Lees promo did its job and I look forward to seeing Lees vs Carnage next month, Caiman vs Paige was a decent match, Paige's character is getting good as are his wrestling skills, nice introduction of Caiman. Sykes vs Dutt was a vicious brawl and the resulting Navarro vs Sykes NO DQ match should be SENSATIONAL! Mensa vs Vaughn had a little trouble following that brawl, it was a solid match, but I have seen both men have better matches.

I think 8 matches is too much for a 2 hour show, with 4 top class matches already announced for December's card it is looking like a can't miss show! Congratulations to LWL on improving their attendance from 62 to 70 this show.

Match of the Night:
LWL National Pride Championship
Mr. Valentino vs Dan Ryder (c)

NOVEMBER 2007 Thoughts

My Live Match of November 2007:
Jimmy Jacobs vs The Bouncer (FCW Anarchy At The Arena 10th November 2007)

My Live Show of November 2007:
Legends Wrestling League 'Winter Warfare' (27th November 2007)

13. December 2007

Triple X Wrestling

Date: Sunday 2nd December 2007
Time: 6:00pm
Attendance: 45
Price: £7
Location: Jolly Beggar, Coventry Skydome,
Coventry, West Midlands.

Ax Title: Defended under 24/7 rules.
Smash Title: Defended under Submission only rules.

Gabriel Grey is your Ring Announcer for the evening.

Pre-Show Madness!

Quentin Hyde Styles and Blok Busta enter the ring. Styles makes Busta the NEW Ax Champion (the fans boo), Spear on Blok Busta is followed by a Rock Bottom by Chris Stone. "Shelf" chant starts up as Jimmy Havoc and Shelf enter the ring. Havoc smacks Busta with Shelf, a drop toe hold follows and finally a jumping DDT on Shelf by Havoc. Havoc puts Shelf on top of Busta and with a 3 count Shelf is the NEW AX Champion!

Well that was FUN! A Good way to start the show, Wrestlers arriving late was an interesting concept that worked really well. Huge cheer for the NEW Ax Champion Shelf who continues to be the biggest star in the entire company! Everybody taking shots at Blok Busta was funny to watch.

Zack Sabre Jr vs Dragon Aisu

Sabre starts the match with a kick to Aisu, who fights back with a kick of his own, chops and forearms are traded as the contest heats up! Sabre catches Aisu in his finishing move (Extended Armbar) but Aisu makes his way to the ropes for the break. Sabre carries on the attack by tripping and quickly applying a wristlock on Aisu. Aisu reverses out, only for Sabre to reverse again into a submission of his own. Aisu counters with a wristlock which Sabre rolls through with a snapmere and then a leg submission of his own!

Sabre KILLS Aisu with a lethal kick to the face that leaves the fans in AWE!! Aisu manages to gather his bearings and low blows Sabre, before hitting a German suplex. The fans chant "Zack, Zack" Aisu connects with another suplex this time a half-nelson one for a close nearfall. Aisu thinks he has it won but Sabre reverses through and back out into a pinfall and with a 1, 2 and 3 picks up the win.

Match Time: 16 minutes

Winner: Zack Sabre Jr

Zack Sabre Jr vs Dragon Aisu = PRO WRESTLING! An absolutely amazing match between two of the best the UK has to offer.

Technically a great wrestling match, strikes from both men were LETHAL, counters and reversals were a sight to behold. 16 minutes of greatness, match of the night unless something amazing happens!

Could be a contender for Match of the Year in the UK also and a definite M.O.T.Y. in Triple X for sure. This match is one which I would put across to any promoter in the world if they want to know why I and many others in the UK believe that Zack Sabre Jr is the very best wrestler the UK has to offer!

Ax Title Madness:
Blok Busta brings out Shelf and with his foot on the ropes pins Shelf to become 2 Time Ax Champion! CK Light comes out with a Frisbee and after throwing it at Busta manages to roll him up to become Ax Champion! The fans chant for "Shelf" once more!

Omer Ibrahim vs Prince Mohammed Ameen

Pre-Match:
When Ameen boasts that he is 3CW Young Lions Champion, Ibrahim talks about how he won his Title in a 137 man tournament.

Match:
Headlock by Ameen, Ibrahim reverses out and knocks Ameen down with a shoulder block. The two competitors trade wrestling holds before a standoff. This quickly ends with comedy, girly slaps, swinging arms and dead legs, all that leaves the TXW fans in hysterics. Both men are down, Ibrahim rises quickest and connects with his patented hand-wash (variation of Samoa Joes face-wash but with his hand). A fisherman's buster follows, as the fans chant for Ibrahim to 'Make him humble.'

Ibrahim responds, "I'm gonna breaka hiss back!" Ameen reverses an Irish whip and clobbers Ibrahim with a Nothern Lariat for a two count. He then demands the fans make noise, they do (booing loudly). Ameen then takes the carpet he brought to the ring and attempts Davari's 'Magic Carpet Ride' but misses allowing Ibrahim time to compose himself and finish the match with his Gore.

Match Time: 5 minutes

Winner: Omer Ibrahim

The pre-match antics were superb! The match was short but contained a lot of fun. First time seeing Ameen but with such a short match apart from saying he has good microphone skills I can't really comment too much on his wrestling ability.

Ibrahim I have seen a few times, he is the cult favourite in Triple X. Having been cheered for, for months on end he finally started playing up to the fans and they love him for it. Great way to follow up a wrestling clinic!

Sidekicks (Andy Shoes & CK Light) vs Martin Kirby & Cameron Kraze

Pre-Match:
Kirby and Kraze make their way to the ring to Celine Dion's 'My Heart Will Go On' complete with Titanic pose in the corner! The fans didn't know whether to laugh or cry when they see this unveiling before their very eyes.

Kraze states. "It's still real to me dammit!" Shoes sees the opportunity for Championship Glory and quickly pins his OWN partner to win the Ax Title. Kirby and Kraze then strategize. "This is a sneak attack waiting to happen."

Match:
Shoes uses the distraction to hiptoss Kirby. Light interjects with a backbreaker but sees his Irish whip reversed and then he is hung on the top rope neck first by Kraze & Kirby. "I'm involved now, you jump, I jump!" Kirby tells Kraze, "This ends badly!" Kraze sheepishly admits. Light connects with an axe handle and a somersault on top of Kirby & Kraze, Kraze gets back to his feet and quickly rakes Light's eyes. The fans show their hatred by throwing beer mats at Kraze & Kirby.

Clothesline, snapmere and senton in quick succession by Kraze but as he attempts the pin Light breaks it up. Shoes nips up and hits Kraze with a clothesline, as Kirby disposes of Light. Shoes powerbombs Kraze and quickly follows up with a Boston Crab, Kraze tries to help Kirby by pulling him towards the ropes. Kirby hilariously shouts, "Let go Cameron!" Kraze reaches the ropes and fires back with a kick to Shoe's head and quickly connects with the Tighe-Tanic for the three count.

Grey confirms that Kraze is the NEW Ax Champion.

Match Time: 9 minutes

Winners: Cameron Kraze & Martin Kirby

Yet another fun match! Highly entertaining from the entrances right through to the end of the match, Kirby and Kraze entering to 'My Heart Will Go On' was a hilarious moment especially with the Titanic pose!

Triple X fans brought the unique and hilarious chants once more which added to the match. The match itself was a good tag with all four competitors having the chance to shine. When all was said and done a NEW Ax Champion was crowned in Cameron Kraze!

Stiro vs Chris Stone vs 'Arriba-Tista' El Ligero

Ligero enters to party poppers and the Triple X roster on bended knee! Being announced by Grey as 'Arriba-Tista.' Ligero shoulder blocks both men down. Stone attacks Ligero from behind, but Ligero uses his obvious power advantage to great effect by breaking through a double clothesline attempt and returning with one of his own. Ligero continues the assault with a shoulder thrust to Stiro and clothesline for Stone.

Wonderwhirl by Stiro, Stone breaks up the pin and connects with a reverse DDT. Ligero fights back with a spear on Stone, Ligero continues the attack with a jackhammer once again on Stone. Ligero then shakes the ropes and points his thumbs down quickly connecting with a sit-down powerbomb but as he attempts a pin Stiro rolls him up and with his hand grasping the ropes picks up the pinfall.

Match Time: 9 minutes

Winner: Stiro

I was wondering if a third predominantly comedy match was overkill, but when El Ligero entered as Arriba-Tista you couldn't help but be entertained. Ligero mimicking Batista's moves and mannerisms was a sight to behold and added great entertainment to what the fans were sure would be good wrestling match.

No doubt Ligero shined but Stone and Stiro put forth good performances in their own right. Stiro picking up the win by cheating leaves the opportunity for a rematch with El Ligero and that is a match I would welcome with open arms.

INTERMISSION including Ax Title Madness Part 2:

Dragon Aisu made his way to the bar where Ax Champion Cameron Kraze was standing, although their meeting was friendly at first Aisu quickly trapped Kraze in a nerve hold. With a referee nowhere to be found Aisu decided to take fan participation to a whole new level by allowing a TXW fan to check the arm as it fell three times with that Dragon Aisu became the NEW Ax Champion!

Masked Man Tournament Qualifying Match

Jekkel vs Exodus

Fans clap for both competitors, in the early going it seems like they know each other's manoeuvres a little too well as it becomes a shadowing contest (with both wrestlers shadowing the others move). Grey is incensed as he expected them to tear each other apart,

Jekkel & Exodus leave the ring to confront Grey and just as they about to put a beating on him, he wriggles out and pushes Exodus into Jekkel.

Jekkel driver only manages a two count, an attempt at a second leads to Exodus countering into a powerbomb for another two count! Exodus looks to have the match won with his swinging Rock Bottom finisher but the Damned Nation appear distracting him... Jekkel takes full advantage by rolling up Exodus for the 1, 2 and 3.

Exodus understands Jekkel's thought process and they shake hands with Exodus raising Jekkel's hand.

Match Time: 7 minutes

Winner: Jekkel

The Masked Man Tournament is the brain child of Damned Nation member Majik, too much of a coincidence for two of his most hated enemies to be facing each other in the first round for my liking. Unfortunately for Majik his plan backfired as although Jekkel won with a pretty cheap finish there didn't seem to be any dissension in the ranks when all was said and done.

The match itself was ok, the shadowing of moves was enjoyable to watch. Both men turning on Grey was great also, and the ending furthers the Damned Nation vs Jexodus feud, so job done.

Edgar Stryfe w/The Boss & John Bull vs Devilman

Devilman announces that this is the first time wrestlers have circled left while starting a match the fans chant, "This is awesome." Stryfe shows his great power advantage over Devilman by pushing him off whilst in a lock-up, Devilman fights back with a kick to Stryfe's head, spin kicking his stomach and connecting with another kick to Stryfe's head.

Boss distracts the Referee, Devilman is wise to this and uses it to hit a clothesline on Stryfe a kick on Bull and a jumping DDT, Bull intervenes and with a powerbomb in front of the Ref which causes the Disqualification.

Match Time: 12 minutes

Winner by Disqualification: Devilman

Good power vs quickness match, Stryfe showed he can be a force to be reckoned with in Triple X especially with his entourage. Devilman showed why he is nicknamed 'Mr Triple X Wrestling' with his resilience in the face of diversity.

A back and forth match, that could have gone either way, the DQ finish may look cheap but from a logical perspective it makes sense. Stryfe couldn't beat Devilman alone so when Bull was aware of that they tried instead to injure Devilman.

Ax Title Madness Part 3:
El Ligero steals Dragon Aisu's 1PW Tag Title and runs into the Triple X ring. Aisu tries to bargain: "Swap." Ligero then uses a Party Popper to shock Aisu into a quick roll up and becomes the NEW Ax Champion.

Smash Title fought under Submission ONLY rules

'Suicidal, Suicidal, Suicidal' Jimmy Havoc vs Majik (c)

Grey knocks Shelf down, Havoc applies a leglock to Majik but Majik is able to reach the ropes for the break. The fans clap, Majik puts Havoc in an armlock setting up for a legsweep before transitioning into the submission. Havoc returns with a backbreaker following this Havoc steals a page out of his Tag Team Partner's playbook (Zack Sabre Jr) by applying an extended armbar. Shoulder thrusts by Majik, into his patented Russian legsweep.

Havoc replies with forearms, shoulder thrusts and a sunset flip. Havoc locks in the Cattle Mutilation "Tap!" chant the fans and although he tried to struggle free Majik couldn't take the pain and tapped out, with that Jimmy Havoc becomes NEW Smash Champion. The fans greet this with chants of, "Jimmy, Jimmy!"

Post-Match:
Quentin Hyde Styles announces that next month it will be Damned Nation vs Jexodus and the losing team can't team ever again in Triple X! He also

cryptically states that a Former American Wrestling Champion will be coming to Triple X in March.

Match Time: 16 minutes

Winner and NEW Smash Champion: Jimmy Havoc (c)

Well I think that was an answer to those who (wrongly in my view) criticized Havoc! Havoc wrestled a more toned down style but this match is proof his technical wrestling skills are not to be sniffed at. He and Majik put forth a good wrestling match based around counters, reversals and counter reversals.

The submission only rules added an interesting element to the match as Havoc is known for his high flying and brawling style, could he really make Majik submit? Majik is a more technical wrestler so you would think this match would play into his hands. Never judge a book by its cover I guess is the lesson to be learned, as Havoc made Majik submit to become the NEW Smash Champion. Good way to end the show!

Ax Title Madness Part 4, 5 and 6:
A boxed person scrambles around the ring led by Ibrahim (it's El Ligero), Ibrahim talks him into laying down and becomes the NEW Ax Champion. Blok Busta makes his way out and after figuring out which hand makes the Claw work submits Ibrahim to become NEW 3 Time Ax Champion. As Blok Busta is making his way to the back Stiro attacks with a Dragon Sleeper and becomes the NEW Ax

Champion. Grey shouts, "100% angry baby!" as the fans chant, "We want more!"

Pre-Show Madness was fun! Sabre Jr vs Aisu was a great advert for Pro Wrestling. Ibrahim vs Ameen was highly entertaining with great microphone work by both men pre-match. Sidekicks vs Kraze & Kirby was a good entertaining tag match, Stiro vs Arribatista vs Stone was a fun comedy match with hilarious moments. Exodus vs Jekkel did its job of continuing Damned Nation vs Jexdous feud, Stryfe vs Devil-Man was a good match in its own right.

Havoc vs Majik was a great way to end the show. Ax Title madness that happened all show long was incredibly entertaining. Triple X without a doubt produces some of if not the very BEST bell to bell wrestling in the UK! It is so frustrating that only 45 fans turned out to see this great night of wrestling action.

Match of the Night:
Zack Sabre Jr vs Dragon Aisu

AWW

Date: Thursday 13th December 2007
Time: 8:00pm
Attendance: 80
Price: £5
Location: Irish Centre, Digbeth, Birmingham, West Midlands.

Stu Smith is your Ring Announcer for the evening.

The Young Gunns (Tommy Gunn & Geraden) vs Nick Knight & 'Human Hate Machine' Moralez

Even though there is an incredible weight advantage for Knight & Moralez the Young Gunns do not back down during the face to face stare down. Moralez takes this opportunity to slap and club Gunn before tagging out to Knight. Knight continues the assault with a stalling powerslam, before he tags Moralez back in. The fans rally behind Gunn with chants of, "Tommy, Tommy!" as a stalling suplex by Moralez garners a two count.

Geraden connects with an Enzuguri to Moralez but the follow up top rope cross body doesn't faze Moralez. Knight saw the opportunity and hit with a spinebuster, Moralez followed that up with a lariat and a vicious club to Gunn before Knight finished the Young Gunns off with a top rope Frog splash.

Match Time: 10 minutes

Winners: 'Human Hate Machine' Moralez & Nick Knight

Good to see Geraden back in AWW and it is good to see the Young Gunns tagging once more. Although this was a more a showcase of what Nick Knight and Moralez can do, the Young Gunns put forth a valiant performance against the much bigger foes.

Had Geraden's high cross body block on Moralez worked the Young Gunns may have won the match, it didn't though and from there Moralez and Knight decimated the two young up and comers.

'Desirable' Danny D vs Kid Glory

Danny jaws with the crowd and steals a Glory sign a fan was holding up, much like at Aston University he rips it up, to the dismay of the Glory fans. The AWW fans go crazy as Glory enters! D offers a handshake which Glory wearily accepts only to be met by a slap by D, D follows up with a fall away slam as the fans chant, "Glory!/Glory!"

Glory fights back with a hurricanrana for a two count. D connects with a powerbomb which he turns into a second before applying the Boston Crab for the submission victory.

Match Time: 3 minutes

Winner: 'Desirable' Danny D

Not much of a match with only 3 minutes time allowed. Kid Glory got a superstar like reaction when he made his way to the ring! Whilst in the ring he showed some potential against the much more experienced Danny D.

D showed that he can back up what he says by making the youngster tap out to the Boston Crab. I'd like to see these two go at it again with a longer time limit in place.

Stu Smith runs down the rest of the card and announces that 'Star Man' Mark Clarke will be taking British Born Steele's place in the triple threat #1 Contenders match.

'The Metro-Sexual' Danny Devine vs Marcus Kool

Pre-Match:
Devine takes the microphone and whilst attempting to talk a fan in the audience shouts him down to which Devine replies, "Shut up! You are Ginger!"

The fans hilariously reply with a, "We love Gingers!" chant.

"At Aston University I nearly broke his leg, I want you to all have a Merry Metro Christmas." Kool walks out limping heavily (still showing the effects of the Aston University show) but when he sees Devine he runs in only for Devine to duck out.

Match:
Kool attacks Devine with chops, fists and clotheslines putting Devine on the defensive right from the start. A Japanese armdrag and back elbow follow as Devine is reeling from Kool's offensive. Kool throws another elbow which Devine blocks using this to spin Kool around so he lands on his bad leg. Devine zeros in on Kool's bad leg with a chop block and continuous kicking before attempting to apply the sharpshooter but Kool has enough strength in his leg to push Devine off.

The fans clap and cheer for Kool as even with a bad leg he attempts to nip up! Devine catches Kool's Superkick and reverses it into a Sharpshooter, Kool struggles but manages to reach the ropes for the break as the fans cheer. Devine holds on and drags Kool back into mid-ring but once again the tenacious Kool reaches the ropes. Devine obviously more content on injuring Kool than actually winning the match refuses to break the hold and the Referee has no choice but to award the win to Kool via a Disqualification.

Match Time: 10 minutes

Winner by Disqualification: Marcus Kool

Aftermath:
Devine continues the assault, "I don't care about his leg," as the Referees try to stop him. Devine picks up a chair from the crowd and with Kool's leg wrapped around the post, slams the chair into it to a sickening cracking noise. Devine satisfied that Kool is done leaves as Tommy Gunn, Geraden and Lee Hunter help Kool to his feet as the fans chant, "We love Marcus!"

That was a superb contest between two of the best AWW has to offer. The kind of match where it doesn't matter who the loser is, as both the winner and loser gain a lot from just participating in the match itself. Kool's resilience was there for all to see as he battled Devine on one good leg.

Devine has shown a more cerebral side of himself in the last few months in AWW and it works for him. Kool vs Devine has been as good as I thought it would be and I for one say LONG may this feud continue.

Mad Man Manson vs 'Jamaica's #1 Bobsledder' Derice Coffie

Coffie asks for the Referee to check Manson's boots! Whilst the Ref checks Manson shouts out, "Touch it again! Oh yeah!" as the hilarity begins. Manson headlocks Coffie and with a shoulder block knocks him down hilariously asking, "Are you alright?" Coffie takes this opportunity to trip Manson and Jamaican Waves for the AWW fans. Manson says he can't breathe and they agree to SLOW the match down! The opening sequence is run through again but this time in slow motion as the fans laugh in hysterics.

Coffie runs up the ropes and connects with a DDT for a two count, Manson fights back with forearms and hits his swinging Rock Bottom on Coffie for another two count. "Only move I've got!" he tells the fans who are still laughing! Manson predicts his own downfall; "Almost always kicks me in the face!" Coffie does just that and finishes the match with a high cross body for the three count.

Match Time: 12 minutes

Winner: 'Jamaica's #1 Bobsledder' Derice Coffie

Well before this match I would have said that nothing could beat Delirious vs Colt Cabana from ROH Liverpool in March, but after watching this match I am now not quite so sure. When it was announced that Manson would wrestle Coffie I knew good things were about to happen.

The slow motion sequence of moves was a joy to behold as the entire Irish Centre laughed out loud. I don't think I have ever laughed so much watching a wrestling match in my entire life! Kudos to both men for bringing some highly entertaining comedy to the card.

Triple Threat Elimination Match for #1 Contendership for AWW Title

Spud vs Dan Ryder vs 'Star Man' Mark Clarke

Pre-Match:
As Spud makes his way to the ring, ripping up a sign and throwing it at the fans. Spud takes the microphone. "The AWW Belt is all mine!" he continues. "It seems like Dan Ryder is #1 Contender because of all the crazy moves he does!" The fans show their support with, "Ryder, Ryder!" chants.

Match:
As the match starts the abuse continues for Spud. "80's reject!" is the fans choice of chant. Clarke and Ryder both attack Spud with double clotheslines. Ryder and Clarke continue the double team as Clarke flicks Ryder into the air for his patented Moonsault for a two count as Spud rolls out. "Me and you," Ryder and Clarke agree, just as they about to fight Spud rolls back in and pushes Ryder into Clarke.

Clarke hits Ryder with a Russian legsweep and a spinning neck breaker but misses the follow up second rope leg drop. Ryder fires back with a dropkick to the face and ascends the turnbuckle, as he does Spud pushes him off. Ryder flies from the turnbuckle almost into the crowd (nearly ten feet away)! With the Referee checking on Ryder, Spud clocks Clarke with his belt and with a Stunner.

Clarke is eliminated 5 minutes into the contest.

The fans rally behind Ryder with chants of, "Let's go, Ryder, let's go," Spud uses this opportunity to stamp on Ryder and illegally choke him. A fish hook follows as he taunts the crowd, "Look at him!" before bellowing out, "Danny Boy!" Ryder fires back and the two competitors trade punches before Spud pokes Ryder in the eye. Ryder fights back once more but is caught by a leg lariat and trapped in a sleeper by Spud.

Spud complains about the count to the Ref, before rushing in and being caught with an overhead throw into the corner by Ryder! 450 maybe… no, Spud pushes Ryder off and connects with a Code Red for a close nearfall. Once again he berates the Ref, setting up for a Stunner - Ryder cleverly reverses into a backslide for the 1… 2… 3! Spud hits back with a Stunner and leaves to more fan abuse as the fans cheer and clap the NEW #1 Contender Dan Ryder!

Match Time: 16 minutes

Winner and NEW #1 Contender for AWW Title: Dan Ryder

That was a very good mixture of entertainment and wrestling. It has gotten to the point where Spud probably doesn't even need to wrestle to attract hatred from the crowd as the AWW fans truly despise him in every sense of the word. Clarke did pretty good as a last minute replacement for British Born Steele.

Ryder showed once more that he isn't out of his league when fighting against the best the UK has to offer. Good match and a very deserving candidate for #1 Contendership to the AWW Title.

Dragon Aisu & Martin Kirby vs Cam Kraze & El Ligero

Pre-Match:
After receiving abuse from the AWW fans Kirby retorts with, "Past your bedtime." He then takes Kraze's hat off his head and stamps on it.

Match:
Strong lock-up between Aisu and Kraze which Kraze wins much to his surprise. "I'm apparently quite strong!" pushing Aisu back into the corner before a clean break. Second time around Aisu wins the lock-up and when asked to break - chops Kraze across the chest. Shoulder block but neither competitor moves at all! Kraze stamps on Aisu's toes and chops Aisu back, before hitting with a Manhattan/Atomic drop combination.

Aisu ends Kraze's offence with an eye poke. Aisu connects with a lariat but Ligero breaks up the pinfall with a dropkick to the head. Aisu chops away at Ligero even turning the chops into Kenta Kobashi like ones. Ligero hits back with a Superkick, Kraze follows up with a Rock Bottom. Kraze then connects with a vicious wonderwhirl onto his knee! Ligero finishes the match with a top rope splash for the three count.

Match Time: 14 minutes

Winners: El Ligero & Cam Kraze

Good tag match between the four guests brought in by AWW. Kirby became an instant target for fan abuse. The match itself was a good showcase for all four competitors. A mixture of comedy and old school tag wrestling produced a fun enjoyable match for the AWW fans.

Stu Smith explains that the next AWW show is on Friday 25th January 2008 and talks of plans to expand into Walsall in 2008.

AWW Title

Lee Hunter vs Carnage (c)

Lock-up into a wristlock by Hunter, Carnage reverses out, Hunter reverses once more this time into a headlock. The reversals continue until Carnage throws Hunter out of the ring, Carnage shows great sportsmanship by allowing Hunter back into the ring. Carnage quickly applies a waistlock but Hunter flips out and returns with a back kick, before applying the wristlock and then an armlock to the AWW Champion.

Both men are down as the fans clap, when back to their feet both men trade punches with Carnage chopping Hunter. Hunter connects with a sunset flip for a two count, both competitors trade a series of pinfall attempts before Hunter locks in a crucifix or so he thought... Carnage skilfully reverses it into his finishing move the Carnage-Bolt for the three count.

Match Time: 10 minutes

Winner and STILL AWW Champion: Carnage (c)

Aftermath:
The fans clap and cheer Carnage as Spud sneaks in with a Steel Chair and clocks Carnage on the back of the head! Dan Ryder runs out and manages to save Carnage from further beat down, Carnage sees Ryder with Chair in hand and thinks (wrongly) that Ryder was the man that hit him, this causes Carnage and Ryder to get into a shoving match. "Did he hit me?" Carnage asks the fans "No it was Spud" the fans reply.

Spud protests his innocence. "I was at the merchandise table buying DVDs, I saw it!" Carnage believes the fans. "I don't believe a word you say!" he shouts at Spud. Carnage and Ryder go back to shoving each other, Ryder has had enough. "I stopped him from caving your head in!" before going face to face with Carnage, finally the tension is broken with a handshake as the show comes to a close.

I enjoyed that match, although the fans were a little bit quiet during the early going. The wrestling was top notch as Hunter proved he could hang with the best AWW has to offer in AWW Champion Carnage (c). Carnage and Hunter wrestled a pretty scientific match with elements of sportsmanship and a great set of nearfalls towards the end.

The finish from the crucifix into the Carnage-Bolt was a thing of beauty and a great way to end the match. The aftermath did a fantastic job of building up anticipation between Ryder and Carnage heading into their Aston University showdown in February 2008!

Young Gunns showed no fear against Moralez & Knight, Glory has lots of fan support. Kool and

Devine is a feud that I hope never ends! Manson vs Coffie was just hilarious, Triple Threat was highly entertaining and had a deserving winner. 3CW guest match was a good old school tag match and Hunter vs Carnage was a good scientific wrestling match with a great finish.

Hunter vs Carnage aftermath built anticipation for Ryder vs Carnage showdown. 80 fans is a pretty good attendance considering the weather conditions on the day. Once again another good show put forth by AWW, a promotion who I feel has the potential to be one of the best in the UK.

Match of the Night:
The 'Metro-Sexual' Danny Devine vs Marcus Kool

Legends Wrestling League

Date: Tuesday 18th December 2007
Time: 7:30pm
Attendance: 58
Price: Adults £5, Kids £3.
Location: Legends Members Club, Oxley Street, Wolverhampton, West Midlands, WV1 1QN.

Motor Mouth Mike is your Ring Announcer for this evening.

Mat Mensa addresses the LWL Fans...
Mensa first thanks the crowd for their support, then he asks the question that has been on everyone's lips since last month: "Why Maxx?"

Before he can get an answer to that question Mr Valentino & Matt Vaughn interrupt. Valentino calls

Mensa's win against Vaughn a fluke and spouts off that Mensa isn't a worthy LWL Champion.

Valentino & Vaughn attack Mensa until Mad Dog Maxx makes his way to the ring, after a few moments of hesitation Maxx attacks Vaughn & Valentino! Maxx then talks of how he & Mensa are from the same town and street and the two shake hands.

That was a good way to start the show, questions needed to be answered after Maxx and Mensa shared a stare down last month. What was on Maxx's agenda? We now know he wants the LWL Title but he also showed a great deal of respect for Mensa. More questions have arisen out of this alliance. The old saying, "Keep your friends close but your enemies closer," maybe something for Mensa to keep an eye on.

LWL National Pride Championship

'The Metro-Sexual' Danny Devine vs Dan Ryder (c)

The fans get behind Ryder from the start with chants of ,"Ryder, Ryder." Ryder responds by reversing into a hiptoss and quickly hitting a Japanese armdrag. Ryder follows up with a Lucha throw. With Devine on the outside Ryder sees an opportunity to be crazy (which of course he takes) but Devine is too quick and moves out of the way as Ryder cannonballs towards him.

Devine dropkicks Ryder's back before calling for Devine-Time, Ryder reverses out into the Michinoku Driver for a two count. Ryder with the momentum powerslams Devine and quickly hits his patented 450 Splash for the three count.

Match Time: 11 minutes

Winner and STILL LWL National Pride Champion: Dan Ryder (c)

That was a good match. Both competitors put forth good performances in a back and forth match which was just what you look for in an opening match.

After watching the match I personally thought that the booker had said, "Go and have a good match nothing more and nothing less," which stopped this match from being great. As with a less restricted time limit Ryder vs Devine normally equals match of the night but alas it wasn't to be on this occasion.

'Mr #1' Jonny Costello & Platinum Paige vs 'Sik' Nik Dutt & Caiman

As one fan claps Costello points out, "Clapping on your own is very embarrassing," so more fans join in. Costello wins the lock-up but as Paige holds Dutt he smacks Paige by mistake. He apologizes and strokes Paige's hair and face, with Paige tagged in the same happens again this time Paige pulls back but Dutt dropkicks him into Costello. Dutt armringers Paige and whilst in a wristlock tags in Caiman, who enters via an axe handle off the top rope.

The fans chant, "Nik, Nik!" with Dutt and Costello exchanging tags to Caiman & Paige respectively. Clotheslines knock Paige and Costello down a funny moment as Costello trips over his flag! A big boot follows but Paige breaks up the pinfall. Caiman connects with his swinging Rock Bottom and then with a Rocket Launcher on Dutt the Dutt/Caiman team pick up the victory.

Match Time: 11 minutes

Winners: 'Sik' Nik Dutt & Caiman

Good follow up match to Ryder & Devine. All four men had time to shine and they did as a good tag match progressed. Caiman/Dutt looked like veteran tag partners who had been tagging for years when in reality this was their first match as a team.
    Costello and Paige brought the old school cheating and comedy to the match with all these elements a good match was seen by the LWL fans.

John Sotello (Jonny Costello) addresses the crowd… "I had cancer, before, I didn't want to say it but unfortunately it might be back. I'm 100% dedicated to Professional Wrestling! I didn't want sympathy, believe me when I say every time I'm in this ring I give you 100%. Thank you very much and I'll see you next time." The fans clap and cheer loudly as Sotello leaves.

Sykes vs Kris Navarro 2

Sykes attacks Navarro before the bell. "Did you hear a bell?" he shouts at the Referee. Sykes clubs Navarro with some vicious forearms as the assault continues, Navarro fires back and whilst in the ascendancy Sykes takes a breather. "You're a chicken!" chant starts up.

Sykes grabs Navarro's leg and bends and twists it in the ropes before RIPPING Navarro's knee pad right off! "You cheer for this?" he taunts the crowd. Navarro fights back with a Crucifix for a two count, as Sykes proceeds to spit water on the fans once more. Two overzealous fans jump in the ring and attack Sykes leading to the Disqualification.

Aftermath:
It was a setup as the two 'fans' are Real Deal Wrestling's Havok and Lee Chaos! Carnage, Joey Syxx & Chandler Scott Lee interrupt as RDW are beating down Navarro. "Told you not to mess with me!" directed at LWL Promoter Matt Stark. "RDW is where the big boys play, we are future legends." Carnage, Syxx & CSL help Navarro to his feet and to the back.

Match Time: 11 minutes

Winner: Sykes by Disqualification through interference.

WOW that was intense! Unlike Sykes vs Navarro 1 which was a wrestling clinic, this was a straight up fight. Sykes and Navarro didn't hold anything back as they fought for the win, Sykes's new toned up attitude makes him even more dangerous than he was before (I didn't think that was possible). Navarro showed why he is the rising star in LWL by putting forth an incredibly resilient performance.

The ending of the match completely got me as I thought it was legit! I have heard much good press about Chaos and Havok so I'm intrigued at how they will do when wrestling in front of my eyes. With no definitive winner in this match I see Sykes vs Navarro 3 happening in the future and I for one CAN'T wait! LONG may this feud continue…

INTERMISSION

Respect Match

'New Age' Kristian Lees vs Carnage

Lees applies the wristlock and taunts Carnage saying, "I'll teach you some respect," that allows Carnage to reverse the hold before Lees reverses once more. Carnage leg trips Lees and applies the headlock before transitioning into a hammerlock. Lees elbows out but Carnage holds on before low bridging Lees over the top rope and to the floor. The fans clap and chant, "Chicken, Chicken!" at Lees, Lees leaves but Carnage drags him back out.

Carnage pulls Lees top over his head and connects with a vicious chop, a lariat and belly to belly suplex follow as Carnage takes control of the match. Carnage climbs the turnbuckle a fan shouts "450" to which Carnage replies "I wish!" instead Carnage hits a slingshot splash for a two count. Lees is able to rally and attempts to jump off onto Carnage, Carnage skilfully reverses into a Carnage-Bolt for the three count.

Match Time: 4 minutes

Winner: Carnage

Good for the four minutes given. Four minutes is not a fair amount of time for a person making their in ring debut, but with that being said Lees looked competitive against the veteran Carnage.

So with that I guess you can say job done, I'd like to see Lees in a longer match next time around, Carnage put forth a good performance for the time allowed.

Matt Vaughn & Mr Valentino vs Mad Dog Maxx & LWL Champion Mat Mensa (c)

Maxx & Mensa knock down Vaughn and Valentino with throat chops, more throat chops down Vaughn. Valentino uses, "He's a big boy he can handle himself," as his excuse for not coming to Vaughn's aid. The double team continues on Vaughn and when Valentino interrupts he gets chopped for his troubles. "That one hurt!" he screams.

Maxx continues the assault with an eye scrape on Valentino. "Mad Dog," chant starts up from the LWL fans. Maxx drops Vaughn before chopping Valentino "I love you Mad Dog" Mensa says before kissing Maxx's head! A double lariat follows on Valentino, after knocking down Vaughn a Doomsday Device connects and with that Mensa and Maxx are the winners.

Match Time: 12 minutes

Winners: Mad Dog Maxx & LWL Champion Mat Mensa (c)

Another good match on a card full of them. Mensa & Maxx co-existed incredibly well, if I was going to compare their situation I would to that of Steve Austin and Shawn Michaels when they were forced to fight against the Hart Foundation in 1997.

Everything is just fine right now as it was for Austin and Michaels but Maxx wants LWL gold and Mensa holds it.

So I can see this being a partnership of convenience before the future LWL Title showdown between the two competitors. I'm not forgetting Vaughn and Valentino who looked like a pretty good tag team in their own right, looking competitive even in losing. If this is the start of an LWL Tag Division there are already 3 or 4 teams to work with and it could be good for the company.

LWL Christmas Cracker Rumble for £500 Check (featuring TGR w/The Boss vs Joey Syxx vs The Gentleman Gigalo vs 'Male Model' Tommy White vs Caiman vs Kristian Lees vs Carnage vs G-Force vs The 'Metro-Sexual' Danny Devine vs LWL Dragon vs DR X vs DR Y vs Kris Navarro vs 'Sik' Nik Dutt vs LWL National Pride Champion Dan Ryder (c) vs Chandler Scott Lee vs Sykes vs Havok vs Lee Chaos vs Platinum Paige)

TGR is eliminated by Syxx, Gigalo is eliminated by White, Syxx eliminates Caiman, Syxx eliminates White, Lees is eliminated by Carnage, Navarro eliminates LWL Dragon, Devine and Paige are eliminated by Sykes, CSL, Dr X and Dr Y are eliminated shortly after, G-Force is thrown out onto Dr X and Y, Ryder and Carnage are also eliminated.

It's down to 3 on 3 - LWL (Syxx, Navarro & Dutt) vs RDW (Sykes, Chaos & Havok). Sykes eliminates Navarro, Chaos and Havok forget about Rumble and concentrate on finishing off Navarro and Syxx! Sykes and Dutt are left one on one, with Sykes in control. Dutt fights back as the crowd explode! Sykes gains control once more. "Who wants him?" but this allows Dutt to connect with a dropkick and Enzuguri to eliminate Sykes and WIN the Christmas Rumble!

It looks like RDW vs Dutt until Syxx & Navarro even up the odds with chairs. RDW leave before Sykes threatens Stark once more. "RDW vs LWL in January elimination tag, book it! You (while pointing at Navarro) I'm going to break your frigging neck!"

Match Time: 26 minutes

Winner of the LWL Christmas Cracker Rumble for £500 Check: 'Sik' Nik Dutt

Well like all Rumbles this was a blink and you might miss it event. Chaotic would be a good way to sum it up, good to see G-Force (aka Geraden) make his debut in an LWL ring. I hope that is a regular occurrence for the young up and comer.

A lot of the near eliminations looked like they were supposed to be eliminations so that was a little sloppy. When it was down to 3 vs 3 the Rumble improved tremendously! The main stories to come out of the Rumble though Dutt being £500 richer and RDW vs LWL and that should be heated come January 2008.

Mensa & Maxx's alliance should be interesting, Ryder vs Devine was good but both are capable of better. Costello & Paige vs Caiman & Dutt was a good tag match, best of luck to John Sotello in his battle with Cancer! Sykes vs Navarro was a fantastic fight! Carnage vs Lees was good for the time given. Mensa & Maxx vs Valentino & Vaughn was another good tag and if it is a prelude to an LWL Tag Division I welcome it.

Christmas Rumble was chaotic, disjointed at times but LWL vs RDW should be heated when it kicks off next month. 58 fans is less than last time but not too bad considering the time of year. LWL has really turned itself into a very good promotion who are beginning to make a name from themselves, long may that continue.

Match of the Night:
Sykes vs Kris Navarro 2

DECEMBER 2007 Thoughts

My Live Match of December 2007:
Zack Sabre Jr vs Dragon Aisu - Triple X 'Jak'd Off' (2nd December 2007)

My Live Show of December 2007:
Triple X (December 2nd 2007)

Match Of The Year – 2007:
45 Minute Iron Man Match for 1PW Openweight Title
Darren Burridge vs Nigel McGuinness (c)

14, WHAT A WAY TO END THE YEAR!

Towards the end of 2007 I started thinking about Wrestlemania 24. With it being Austin's Homestate, was there a way for me to make a Life Long dream come true!? We looked at all of the variables and decided we could make it work!

2008 would finally be the year when my Life Long dream of attending a Wrestlemania Live (Wrestlemania 24) would come true, but that is a story for another time…

Thank you for reading, I hope you have enjoyed my book.

ABOUT THE AUTHOR

Oliver Newman has been a Professional Wrestling Fan for 25 Years and a Writer for 12 Years. He lives in the West Midlands, England, United Kingdom.

Comments/Questions/Feedback please feel free to contact/interact with him on:

Twitter: twitter.com/brummieol
Facebook: facebook.com/afansperspectiveuk
Email: a-fans-perspective@outlook.com

For more of his work be sure to check out – a-fans-perspective.16mb.com - A Fan's Perspective on the World of Professional Wrestling – for the Fans by a Fan.

Printed in Great Britain
by Amazon